"*Gaslighting for God* is laugh-out-loud funny, which is great for those of us who've survived religious trauma and need to laugh it out sometimes, so we're not always crying. But don't let Garison's clever wit fool you—this book is also a deep and sharply insightful commentary on narcissistic leadership, including valuable and practical ways to spot a predator in pastoral clothing."

—Tia Levings, author of the NYT Bestselling *A Well-Trained Wife: My Escape from Christian Patriarchy* and *I Belong to Me: A Survivor's Guide to Recovery and Hope after Religious Trauma*

"Becky Garrison's *Gaslighting for God* is not only deeply researched, it's also deeply felt, a wise and knowing exposé of religious narcissists in what she calls the Christian Industrial Complex—and beyond. Her taxonomy of narcissists manages to be both funny and frightening, but the real treasure of this book lies in its promise of hope and healing, courage found in the context of community."

—Randall Balmer, author of *Bad Faith: Race and the Rise of the Religious Right*

"Becky is, among other things, a historian who has kept close watch over what has happened through different church movements over the last few decades. She is duly qualified to comment, sometimes with sarcasm, about the patriarchy and gaslighting that help keep their followers in line. If we are ever going to move forward out of evangelical Christianity, we need fair criticism of the current situation and the methods used by those who rule and manipulate. This book will accomplish that!"

—Karl Forehand, author of *Evolving from Religious Trauma* and host of *The Desert Sanctuary*

"While we may not align with all of the author's claims, *Gaslighting for God* is a needed voice in a time when self-anointed gurus sell salvation like merch. Becky Garrison cuts through the fog with a sly grin and a sharp pen. She exposes how narcissists, whether in pulpits, on stages, or leading 'sacred' movements and retreats, twist faith into fuel for their own empires. With honesty and humor, she documents the red flags and provides a way out, pointing us toward spaces where spirituality heals instead of harms. It's part exposé, part survival guide—a much-needed invitation to reclaim our own sacred path."

—David Hayward, a.k.a the NakedPastor, cartoonist and author

"Ever wonder why the church seems to focus more on the minister than the mission? *Gaslighting for God* by Becky Garrison will help you understand why so many churches focus on glitz rather than God and elevate people's egos over religious purpose. Garrison uses in-depth research and witty satire to expose religious narcissism in this engaging volume."

—Warren Throckmorton, author of *The Christian Past That Wasn't: Debunking the Christian Nationalist Myths That Hijack History*

"*Gaslighting for God* offers a clear and incisive examination of the narcissistic dynamics that shape harmful religious environments. Becky Garrison names what so many experience but rarely have language for. As a nursing scholar and researcher of adverse religious experiences, I see this book as an important contribution to our understanding of spiritual trauma and the pathways to recovery."

—Beth K. Schwartz, PhD, RN, PHN, MAT

"Countless resources shine light on dark details of malignant individuals and institutions. But Becky Garrison uniquely equips us with her master class in surgical satire. *Gaslighting for God* pokes holes in their persona puffery, unmasks their manipulations, and defangs their Medusa snakes of disinformation. Essential reading to understand and defend against spiritual narcissism!"

—Brad Sargent, abuse survivor blogger at *futuristguy*

Gaslighting for God

Gaslighting for God

A Satirical Guide to Save Yourself
from Spiritual Narcissists

Becky Garrison

lakedrivebooks.com

Lake Drive Books
6757 Cascade Road SE, #162
Grand Rapids, MI 49546
info@lakedrivebooks.com
lakedrivebooks.com
@lakedrivebooks
Publishing books that help you heal, grow, and discover.

This book is not intended as a substitute for the medical advice of physicians or as a replacement for therapy with a licensed mental health professional. The reader should consult a physician in matters relating to their health and particularly with respect to any symptoms that may require diagnosis or medical attention.

This book includes personal stories. It reflects the author's present recollections of experiences and information gathered over time. Some names and characteristics have been changed, some events have been compressed, and some dialogue has been re-created.

All scripture quotations are taken from The Holy Bible, New International Version®, NIV® Copyright © 1973, 1978, 1984, 2011 by Biblica, Inc.® Used by permission. All rights reserved worldwide.

Paperback ISBN: 978-1-957687-70-4
E-book ISBN: 978-1-957687-71-1
Library of Congress Control Number: 2025918200

Cover design by Jonathan Sainsbury. 6 x 9 Design
Author photo by thor.pdx

Warning:

This book contains depictions of extreme spiritual narcissism that may be disturbing to critical thinkers.
Reader discretion is advised.

Contents

Introduction: Spiritual Narcissists Among Us

In 1994, I thought I had found my calling as a religious satirist when I sold my first article to *The Wittenburg Door*, at the time the world's largest, oldest, and only Christian satire magazine. After rising to the rank of senior contributing editor, *The Door* slammed in my face when it closed shop in 2008.

By the time I moved to the Pacific Northwest six years later, I had stopped calling myself a professional Christian. The Christian media industry (nicknamed the "Christian Industrial Complex" by author Warren Cole Smith, among others)[1] had imploded under the weight of its unholy hubris. Believers were fleeing from institutional churches like rats from a sinking ship, myself included. With limited employment opportunities in the Bible biz, I said to myself, "I'm done satirizing this God game." I could see the writing on the wall: the institutional church was going under, Titanic-style, with no lifeboats in sight.

Cutting-edge ventures aimed at rebranding the church as "cool" used to draw in those disenchanted with traditional forms of institutional church, but these methods no longer appealed to twenty-first-century pious peeps. The liberal mainline Episcopal Church of my youth that once marched in solidarity with Martin Luther King, Jr., was now walking biblically bowlegged, so to speak (sans a few prophetic outliers like Manhattan-based St. Mark's Church-in-the-Bowery).

Conversely, conservative forms of religion, appealing to many, were appalling to many more, many of whom said they were "done" with religion and went on to live entirely secular lives. Once these people stop checking off the correct Christian category, the institutional church drops them from their membership list as though they committed a serious spiritual sin. Some religion writers call these secular people "nones" because that's what they put on the census forms under "religion."

In my reporting on American Christianity, I observed how these "nones" and "dones" felt free to choose a path that spoke to them, one without guilt-ridden dogmas. Some find occasional comfort in a church, synagogue, temple, or mosque that truly welcomes all, one that aims to be a place of healing, not a means of harm to others. Others choose to worship, reflect, or meditate outside of traditional religious structures. Simultaneously, for the first time in U.S. history, atheists began to come out of the closet in droves.[2]

I had to wonder why more and more people were distancing themselves from religious institutions. Soon enough, through my ongoing connections with trauma experts and survivors of spiritual abuse, I became increasingly aware of how spiritual narcissists have dominated the American Christian culture I had been satirizing since I penned my first piece for *The Wittenburg Door* back in 1994. Even though I could now see some patterns emerging that helped explain this dynamic, I had no viable outlets where I could place these stories other than the infrequent piece for *Spirituality & Health*. I now had the tools I needed to make at least some sense of this missional madness, but it seemed no one else was interested.

However, when I got word in 2021 that *The Door* was reopening in an online format, I agreed to serve on the Board of Directors, hoping this development was more than just a blessed blip. Then, in 2022, I began writing for the humanist online platform *OnlySky*.

Here I focused on covering sex, including #churchtoo abuses, and drugs (cannabis and psychedelics) for their Taboo section. But within a year the site went dark due to a lack of funding. I had to assume my second life as a religious satirist was just a fad and not the start of something bigger.

And then—surprise!—*OnlySky* reemerged in a restructured format in conjunction with a burgeoning interest by other outlets in works reporting on #metoo abuses within supposedly sacred settings. Concurrently, a #churchtoo tsunami invaded the shores of my social media feeds. All these developments told me that perhaps, just maybe, I needed to dip my toe back into this God game.

So here I am, back and barefoot.

This time I'm returning as an outsider without the label of "Christian author," though even during my twenty-five-year stint as a religious satirist, I was never Bible-blessed enough to morph into a *New York Times* bestselling, branded Christian celebrity. Seems I've been on the outs from the get-go.

© NakedPastor

With *Gaslighting for God: A Satirical Guide to Save Yourself from Spiritual Narcissists,* I shift from satirizing those Christian leaders who put profit over prophecy to viewing these charismatic charlatans through the lens of spiritual narcissism. The title of this book stems from the blowback I get whenever I call someone's not-so-sacred sh*t on the carpet. For as long as I can remember, my B.S. detector has a propensity to go into overdrive whenever I encounter an individual or institution that gives me a case of the unholy heebie jeebies. Even when I can't quite identify the specific reasons why I'm getting these somatic sensations, I've learned over the years to trust my gut when something feels amiss.[3]

This inner intuition, coupled with the intense desire to speak truth to pastoral power that I inherited from my twelfth-great-grandfather Roger Williams (a seventeenth-century religious freedom pioneer), led me to become a religious satirist. The same instincts also informed me when it was time to leave the institutional church and become a traveling pilgrim just like my ancestor. In this journey I went from calling myself a pre-natal Episcopalian (do the ecclesiology and the science), courtesy of my late Episcopal priest/sociology professor father, to describing myself as an apophatic agnostic Anglican.

I can still trace what the Celts called the thin line separating this world from the next as I embrace both the Cloud of the Unknowing and my Anglican heritage—but I'll break out in unholy hives if I'm forced to sit on a hard wooden pew surrounded by even more hardened, knotty souls. I'm more liable to encounter the divine while kayaking or fly-fishing down a river, camping surrounded by the Douglas Firs that serve as my cathedral, walking along the Pacific Northwest's ragged coastline, getting lost in a spirit-filled festival, or celebrating with my chosen community at my local cidery, brewpub, or tasting room.

> Every day people are straying away from the church and going back to God.
>
> —Lenny Bruce[4]

Yet my B.S. detector kept going off whenever I was in the presence of "enlightened" energies such as tantra pujas, ecstatic dances, and mindfulness meditation circles—especially those with a bastardized Buddhist bent. Why was I so drawn to these supposedly welcoming and inclusive spiritual settings that brought me to a state of bliss but also kept triggering me?

My search for answers to this question began after I connected with a licensed (supposedly trauma-informed) therapist at these happenings and our professional and personal relationship imploded in 2016.[5] Thanks to a narcissistic abuse support group I joined shortly thereafter, I realized this person possessed personality traits found among those who possessed extreme narcissistic traits. Whenever I found myself surrounded by narcissistic energies, my mind might have believed that I should depart from this setting, but my body didn't behave. So I stayed. Gradually I developed the self-awareness and ability needed to keep my triggers under control. Yet I still felt an overwhelming anxiety hiding behind my Southern smile whenever I was in a narcissism-riddled scenario that didn't sit well with my soul. In my attempts to keep my anxiety at bay, I would talk through my discomfort, a dynamic that too often made people think I was self-centered by hogging the conversation when I was feeling self-conscious instead.

Finally, I found healing from my childhood traumas via somatic therapies on the advice of another allegedly trauma-informed therapist I met during my reporting on the Portland sex-positive community. Surprise, surprise, this therapist proved to be cut from the same narcissistic cloth. But something told me that despite meeting two therapists who did not practice what they preached, I needed to find a way to fully release my traumas from my past and stop carrying this leftover luggage with me into the future.

Unpacking My Trauma Baggage

When I began to unload my sacramental suitcase, I found myself struck with a sudden case of devotional diarrhea. Why in god or goddess's name did I ever hang on to these theological trinkets thinking they were all golden and good? Even if I chuck this ungodly garbage, how do I get rid of this sacrosanct stench that won't go away no matter how many times I cleanse myself? Is it possible for me to take a more breathable and believable backpack with me in my spiritual journey?

In my attempts to answer these questions, I've become acquainted with the latest research in narcissism and trauma. Also, I've explored somatic modalities used to help heal those impacted by abuses inflicted by spiritual leaders possessing extreme narcissistic tendencies. This work has greatly informed my writing as a religious satirist as it allows me to understand why some self-anointed spiritual masters both woo and wound others.

Key to this interplay is the concept of "charisma." We tend to think of certain people as having a charismatic magnetism that draws people to them. But this appears to be a chicken-or-the-egg dilemma. Are certain people innately imbued with a particular appeal? Or as sociologist Max Weber (1864–1920) argued that charisma is not a quality of a person but an attribute (of 'power') that is bestowed on someone by others.[6] Given the extremely limited work I can find exploring the dynamics of those who possess charisma and also score high on the narcissism scale, more research needs to be done in this regard.

As I delved into the growing mound of resources about #churchtoo and other forms of spiritual abuse, I noticed a particular pattern starting to emerge: survivor stories give hope to others suffering from missional mistreatment by letting them know they are not alone and that recovery is possible. These books can be highly instructive, provided the author has recovered enough from their traumas so that they can tell their tale without inflicting further pain on themselves and others. If not, they tend to come off as wounded *un*healers, to put it kindly.

Yes, when re-reading some of my earlier musings on religion in America, I can see how I too came off as a bit Christian cray-cray. Even though I don't have a diagnosed mental illness, my over-the-top anxiety would spring up whenever I found myself in spiritual situations filled with narcissistic energies. Such spaces re-triggered my childhood traumas caused by growing up in an extended family that loved their liquor with some of them also loving their Lord.

Thanks to the growing awareness around #churchtoo abuses, an increasing number of people know something is amiss at their given place of worship. But until recently, they couldn't identify the dynamics behind their discomfort. Once survivors develop the awareness that their seemingly enlightened experiences were abusive, not angelic, books on religious trauma can help give them the tools they need to begin healing from toxic religious settings. The discernment gleaned from such reading will prove to be vital as they sift through the plethora of resources promoting "spiritual healing." In my reporting on wellness and sacred sexuality spaces, I've seen ample signs of woo-woo weirdness, uncredentialed crud, and even licensed clinical therapists who weaponize their training in pursuit of their own desires over addressing the needs of those under their care. Fortunately, there is a growing mound of books penned by credible sources who have been tackling the latest research into religious trauma, and they have begun to publish constructive content.

However, I don't see much in terms of a practical how-to guide to deal with those instances when your spidey sense goes into overdrive and you feel something is terribly wrong. Even when you realize you're dealing with someone whose behavior seems to go well beyond your garden-variety theological twit or smarmy shaman, you can't quite put your finger on why you're having such a strong gut reaction toward a certain person or setting.

Half of the harm that is done in this world
Is due to people who want to feel important.
They don't mean to do harm—but the harm does not interest them.
  Or they do not see it, or they justify it
Because they are absorbed in the endless struggle
To think well of themselves.

—T. S. Eliot, *The Cocktail Hour*[7]

How can anyone exude this Chakra or Christlike charm in public while lashing out Lucifer-like the nanosecond something doesn't go their way? On the one hand, you know how speaking out against their spectral sh*t will most likely get you kicked to the curb where you can sit with the other missional misfits, but you also know you'll lose your sanity if you continue walking around on eggshells knowing any missteps on your part could awaken their inner spiritual narcissist.

What are the signs that a divine leader has gone from being a pied piper drawing people toward the light to yet another spiritual shill out for their own self-aggrandizement and personal gain? And why in god or goddess' name do people flock to such unpastoral P. T. Barnums?

Gaslighting for God will begin to answer these questions by identifying the narcissistic tendencies I've witnessed in my capacity as a religious satirist over the decades reporting on unholy hucksters. I will examine those placed in positions of power within Christian and other spiritual settings who lack any self-awareness regarding their inability to express genuine empathy or compassion toward others, as well as the planet as a whole.

For those who feel they could never entangle themselves in this web of lies and strange behaviors, Thomas Erikson, author of *Surrounded by Narcissists: How to Effectively Recognize, Avoid, and*

Defend Yourself Against Toxic People, reminds us that narcissists seek out people who are their opposites: "We are empathic, and we want the best for others. Our hearts, if you will, are too big. We feel compassion for the weak, we possess emotional intelligence, and we have genuine confidence, which the narcissists can't emulate."[8] Even if you are turned off by a narcissist's moves, unfortunately, they may be all too interested in attaching themselves to you by charming the pants off you figuratively, and sometimes literally. The more empathetic you are toward them, the more the subtlety of their tactics may leave you wondering what hit you.

I hope this book will aid those interested in exploring their spirituality in identifying the spiritual narcissists in their midst by giving twenty-first-century spiritual seekers the tools to not only survive but thrive when confronting these destructive energies. I will also touch on those who have left Christianity and see how they are subjected to the same toxic institutional dynamics. Then, I will offer signs of healthy spiritual communities led by those with the capacity to demonstrate true empathy. Finally, I will provide a list of resources for those harmed by spiritual abuses so they can explore how to help themselves heal from their wounds.

My dual MDiv/MSW degree from Yale Divinity School and Columbia University's School of Social Work coupled with my work for *The Wittenburg Door, Spirituality & Health,* and other spiritual outlets might make me uniquely suited to diagnose spiritual narcissists. However, I will not play armchair analyst. For starters, I'm a religious satirist, not a licensed social worker. My calling is to serve as a guide for those seeking authentic spiritual communities by speaking truth to power through the vehicle of satire.

Hence, I have zippo interest in joining the growing hordes of self-appointed holy hucksters marketing themselves as religious trauma/narcissism experts and other Oprah-esque therapeutic trash.

And don't get me started on the devotional drivel that passes these days for spiritual self-help. Yes, there are a few diamonds in the rough, but most of what's out there ranges in quality from cubic zirconia to TikTok trinkets. Almost without exception these works should be reclassified in the fiction section, or better yet used as kindling where they can at least do some bit of good. Pass me the Pepto. Please.

My one bit of advice for those who wish to delve into the growing body of work focusing on narcissism and trauma (especially spiritual narcissism and religious trauma) is caveat emptor: let the buyer beware. Yes, it's ironic for an author to pen a book on this topic while encouraging readers to be mindful of their media consumption. But skim through the hordes of material on these topics, and you'll see how much of it is indeed schlock in desperate need of an editor, let alone a proper peer-review process.

Too often in our current cancel culture the word "narcissist" gets tossed about casually, akin to how the Christian church and other spiritual sorts throw around words like "godly," "enlightened," and "believer." In most cases, these pseudo-psychologists are referencing people who have an overly inflated and self-centered sense of self, not those who would fit the clinical definition for narcissism. I will attempt to do better by defining my terms: Throughout this book, whenever I use the word "narcissist," I use it as shorthand for those instances I see signs of specific behaviors common among those who possess extreme narcissistic tendencies to the point that their work harms rather than heals.

Once I've outlined the basic tenets of narcissism, I will unpack the unique dimensions of spiritual narcissism. What makes this particular form of narcissism pernicious not pastoral? I will leave the actual clinical diagnosis of Narcissistic Personality Disorder (NPD) to those licensed therapists who are treating specific clients.

This will be followed by a compact guide to the various types of spiritual narcissists: exhibitionist, grandiose, royal, victim, seductive, communal, and malignant. To aid spiritual pilgrims in spotting spiritual narcissists, I will note their particular identifying markers, where they are found, and how to best approach them. Similar to a field guide that helps wilderness explorers identify healthy versus poisonous plants, this guide will delve into each type of narcissist using the categories used in the contemporary literature focusing on narcissism. By "literature," I mean works penned by clinical therapists and others with actual expertise in this topic—none of this dubious diagnosing performed by a TikTok therapist.

Once spiritual seekers can ascertain when a particular setting does not bode well for their soul, I will offer hope for healing to recover from such egregious energies. While I acknowledge one can find abuses within any global religious or spiritual institution, I focus most of this book on U.S.-based #churchtoo abuses that continue to rock the Christian Industrial Complex. When applicable, I will touch on spiritual movements that attract those leaving Christianity who now find themselves repeating this spiritual spin cycle.

A key reason why this faith-based feculence continues is that those at the high end of the spiritual narcissism scale present a charismatic and compassionate facade that draws in their followers to hop on board their Missional Magical Mystery Tour. Their events are a helluva lot more fun when compared to your typical Sunday Service or boring Buddhist-lite lectures that too often come off as pruny, not praiseworthy. But should a whistleblower stand up and try to bring a particular spiritual icon's darkness into the light, inevitably this sacred soul's more sinister side will emerge, Tasmanian Devil–style.

On a personal note, this research enabled me, too, to see how my prior traumas led me to lash out whenever those self-appointed

Christian leaders and other spiritual sorts demeaned and demonized me when I questioned why their moves were commercialized, not Christlike. Since acquiring this knowledge coupled with somatic therapy (in my case EMDR [Eye Movement Desensitization and Reprocessing]) did the trick,[9] I've learned to depersonalize such spiritual slams and can now call out such ungodly gook without allowing the impact of their toxic theology to enter my body.

When I converse with others about these discoveries, I've noticed how they had similar ah-ha moments once they learned they were not the problem for speaking out when they observed something was amiss. Like me, they were in spiritual settings that left them drained and damaged.

How can we discern if a spiritual setting is mercurial and monied instead of, well, you know, just messy like Mike Yaconelli? More importantly, once we extricate ourselves from such a setting, how can we avoid re-entering similar spiritual spaces led by nefarious narcissists? Consider the manufactured messages offered by those trying to market themselves as the latest, greatest Christian Crusader, Tantra Titan, or some other monied moniker. Upon closer examination, their impact-driven marketing plan proves to be yet another attempt to garner enough social media hype so they can keep on pushing their fabricated fluff.

In the past, whistleblowers and survivors of narcissistic abuse were silenced by these missional manipulators via their "hedge of protection." This unspiritual shrubbery included such pernicious devices as NDAs, cease-and-desist summons, quasi-independent investigative agencies, crisis PR managers, and mandatory mediators, as well as the power of online media and fanatical fan bases to squelch any critiques. Along those lines, some self-proclaimed #churchtoo whistleblowers have their own abusive histories, as well as engaging in selective reporting that fails to address abuses in more progressive Christian settings.[10]

There's no spiritual swashbuckler on the horizon coming down the pastoral pike to rescue us, a la Westley from *The Princess Bride*. But lest we fall into a Pit of Despair, I see signs of hope on the horizon that have the potential to heal those affected by spiritual abuse. All signs point to a shift in public perception toward spiritual abuses as news cycles spew forth a steady stream of stories focusing on spiritual leaders caught buck nekkid—figuratively and at times literally. As expected, when confronted with their malicious misdeeds, these blasphemous bastards tend to go gonzo, irreligious rabbits caught in a Christian cage.

Thanks to the growing body of research into religious trauma and narcissism, we can learn how to avoid such toxic energies while we seek out places where we can not only survive but thrive on our spiritual journeys. Once we become aware whenever an individual, community, or even an entire institution exhibits signs of extreme narcissism, we can learn to walk away from those situations, even if they present themselves as healing oases filled with living water. When we step in a bit too deep, we realize they're contaminated cesspools containing god or goddess only knows what. But once we leave behind that spiritual stench, we can seek out actual living water that can truly transform us and connect us together in our shared humanity.

Can localized grassroots movements bring about a global shift toward transformational change? Or will these sparks of hope crystallize into yet another institutional model that will elevate some while repressing others? Time will tell, but we'll never know if we don't at least try.

But before we all come together to hold hands and sing Kumbaya (on second thought, maybe not), we have some collective healing to do. I hope this guidebook will lead to a greater understanding of the dynamics behind spiritual narcissism so folks can react in healthy ways whenever they meet those who blow off the Buddha, cash in their chakras, or bastardize the Beatitudes. Unless we choose to live a hermit lifestyle or blindly inhabit a biblical bubble that's more influencer- than inspiration-driven, we will continue to be impacted by these energies as we pursue our spiritual paths.

So think of this book as a can of religious Raid, an evangelistic extermination device that can help rid your soul of those Christian cockroaches, spiritual snakes, and other venomous vermin that have infested too many spaces to the point that such dwellings are no longer holy or even habitable.

The long painful history of the Church is the history of people ever and again tempted to choose power over love, control over the cross, being a leader over being led. Those who resisted this temptation to the end and thereby give us hope are the true saints. One thing is clear to me: the temptation of power is greatest when intimacy is a threat. Much Christian leadership is exercised by people who do not know how to develop healthy, intimate relationships and have opted for power and control instead. Many Christian empire-builders have been people unable to give and receive love.

—Henri Nouwen, *In the Name of Jesus:*
Reflections on Christian Leadership[11]

Extreme Narcissism Bingo[12]

Before we delve into the nuances of narcissism, here's a friendly bingo game designed to help you assess if a given "difficult" spiritual sage is a prickly personality or a full-blown narcissist. If you can't get to bingo, odds are you're dealing with the former. But when dealing with someone at the extreme end of the narcissistic spectrum, expect to yell out "bingo" multiple times.

Protector in public but predator in private	It's YOUR fault they're so self-absorbed	Thinks "love" is a four-letter swear word	Revenge served cold is their favorite dish	Emotional regulation button is broken
Saves money on electricity bills by gaslighting	Dares to discipline others but crumbles when critiqued	Their plagiarism checker keeps backfiring	Must be #1 dominant alpha dog	Filled with fantasies of their fabulousness
Favorite hobby is fishing for compliments	Magical ability to transform conversations into monologues	FREE (Kinda, sorta)	Thinks their spiritual sh*t smells like sunflowers	Exploits others' weaknesses for fun and profit
Diet consists of anything that feeds their ego	Skillful seduction followed by ghastly ghosting	Uses charm and cash to cover up crimes	Becomes a rageaholic when told "no"	Must win at all costs even when playing kiddie games
Worships themselves as their own god	Treats people like possessions	Believes boundaries are B.S.	Puts smartphone on selfie mode 24/7	Loves to play the shame game

1
What's the Big Deal About Narcissism?

Every day I open my social media feed, I'm swimming in some sacrilegious sea surrounded by self-appointed spiritual sorts. Increasingly they seem to be pawning off narcissism as a virtue by humblebragging, "We're all a bit narcissistic," with their faithful followers responding with gleeful abandon, "Yes! Yes! Yes! I love narcissists!"

Look, I get this unholy hype. After all, I grew up with the message that I could teach the world to sing, courtesy of Coke and Christ. From *Mad Men* to missiology, we live in a world that glorifies the selfie and rewards us based on how well we are liked and followed. The late cultural critic Neil Postman was indeed spot on in his observations that we are "amusing ourselves to death."[1]

But there's a key difference between dealing with an oversized ego that in Grinch fashion is perhaps a few sizes too big but can be brought down to size on occasion and trying to breathe after someone not only sucks all the oxygen out of the room but also takes away our oxygen mask. Whenever *The Wittenburg Door* would satirize a given individual or ministry, those with healthy egos would welcome the critique. At least on the surface, these spiritually savvy sorts appeared to be willing to acknowledge their role in the whole Jesus for Sale racket.[2] They knew they had made it as a Christian thought leader when the religious satirists started coming after them. Some like Jerry Jenkins, co-author of the *Left Behind* series and one of our favorite targets, actually agreed to sit down with me for a *Door* interview.[3]

Others let their narcissistic flag fly once they got under the glare of the media spotlight. Getting blocked by unbiblical bullies became par for the course for me. The truly god-awful remarks I relished, such as the email I got from the late televangelist Fred Price's assistant, who asked me how I'd like to be burned alive in hell for daring to critique Price's prosperity gospel excesses. She gave me the option of being fried or baked, but as a former Southerner, I'd have to go with a good ol'-fashioned BBQ.[4]

A messianic monster I met a few times too many left me feeling so gross and ungodly that I had to take a cold shower afterward. In hindsight, I regret not doing more to alert the public about his egregious excesses. But at that time, he came off as just one of many bestselling bullies who seemed to be getting a bit too big for their Bible britches. I had no clue he would morph over time into a bogus Bonhoeffer braggadocio, a William Wilberforce wingnut, and Trump's theological toadie.[5] Kind of makes me wonder what exactly else he was cooking when he was writing for *Veggie Tales*.

Other comments induced eye rolls and slight giggles, like the time a tattooed theologian turned bestselling badass messaged me, "You're mean" after it was drawn to their attention that those in the tattoo community don't mention their tats in their bios. Yep, it's that ol' "pot meets kettle" dealie, as though somehow name-calling would magically erase all the decades of on- and offline abuse this public persona unleashed upon others, especially those in the LGBT community, not to mention their constant efforts to remake their devotional dreck so they can keep selling spiritual schlock.

I learned to ignore such spiritual slams, knowing ad hominem attacks are part and parcel of being a religious satirist. For the most part, that is. I did freak out a bit when the Abortion TV folks attempted to locate my personal information in their quest to establish a Nuremberg list of journalists whose coverage of the extremist pro-life movement was not to their liking. Fortunately, the list never materialized, though this encounter led me to start enacting online safeguards to hopefully keep those touting faith-based firearms from using me as theological target practice.

What kept me going were the spiritual pilgrims I encountered when I began writing for *The Wittenburg Door*. My work attracted a mass of like-minded folks who loved Jesus but hated how the American church marketed and monetized his message. After all, 1994 marked not only the year I became a professional religious satirist but also that time when Newt Gingrich, Ralph Reed of the Christian Coalition, and other Religious Right devotees took over Congress. Those Christians who were outraged at their dastardly desecration of Jesus's teachings took delight whenever I'd sling my arrows at the Christian Industrial Complex and its kissing cousin, the institutional church.

Then Jim Wallis's book *God's Politics* became a bestseller in 2005 along with the proliferation of progressive movements such as Emergent Village, Red Letter Christians, and Faithful America. These groups marketed their version of that elusive evangelical elixir guaranteed to magically reimagine the crusty church into a crunchier community. Less god, more granola. Next thing you knew, those select few progressive elites elevated in the media spotlight as the latest and greatest holy hipsters proved to be just as thin-skinned as their conservative (and better coiffed, I might add) Christian counterparts. The more I satirized the faux progressive church, the more I felt my body recoiling from the un-Christlike comments that came from those I once considered to be my peers. (My use of the word "faux" is a deliberate choice as a cursory review of their funding streams revealed that while they might talk an inclusive talk, they took money from some rather dubious sources, to put it kindly.)[6]

Whenever one of these blessed bullsh*tters developed enough of a following that they began to garner some biblical buzz beyond their echo chamber, I'd satirize them as I would anyone who got a bit too big for their Bible britches. I knew I hit my target when these supposedly sacred cash cows mooed. I get that they weren't amused. We all have unique sensibilities, and some just don't find satire entertaining. But their responses went well beyond simply agreeing to disagree. They spearheaded cyberbullying campaigns, demanded that my editors take a piece down or give me the axe, and called me names like degenerate, wingnut, and mentally ill. These progressive posers seemed to be unaware that using terms like "mentally ill" as derogatory slurs represents a major slam to those souls who do their damnedest to manage their mental health. So much for promoting oneself as a progressive thought leader; they acted more Neanderthal than nurturing.

By this point in my professional writing career, I had developed a pretty thick skin and cobbled together a supportive community, which helped keep me focused on the prize. Still, I felt soul-slammed when a person I thought was an ally proved to be pompous once they got under the glare of the media spotlight. How did a fellow companion on the journey who once welcomed me with open arms prove to be so vicious once they got a taste of public notoriety?

Despite my attempts at spiritual direction, therapy, and a range of self-help modalities, these questions remained unanswered. Even though I had dealt successfully with the aftereffects of my extended family's history of alcoholism, why was I getting triggered by these spiritual slams? Also, what made my targets so touchy?

Then, in 2008, I began penning *Jesus Died for This? A Satirist's Search for the Risen Christ*, a book that happened to mark my last work for the explicitly evangelical Christian market. As part of my research for the book, I discovered writer and comedian Merrill Markoe's writings on narcissism.

Markoe describes narcissists as people who "cover up feelings of shame and worthlessness inflicted during their own screwy child-hoods by doing whatever it takes to maintain a false sense that they are very special and therefore not bound by ordinary rules." She offers an insightful explanation for why people like most of my extended family, many of *The Door's* theological targets, and my progressive former peers tend to act in this manner:

> Narcissists need to live in a world that is one person big because they never fully outgrow a phase of infantile behavioral development in which Baby thinks he and Mommy are the same person . . . When you are with a narcissist, *their* needs must become your needs . . . It's not enough for a narcissist to be the center of their own world; they must be the center of your world as well.[7]

As I recounted in *Jesus Died for This?* those with extreme narcissistic tendencies like my Episcopal priest and sociology professor father, imbued with the spirit of self-righteousness, deceive themselves into believing their desires are in sync with God's plans for their lives. The Lord's Prayer asking God that "Thy will be done" is replaced by "My will be done" or "God bless my will."[8] Eventually I stopped serving as Dad's altar girl once this once visionary priest became so blind drunk, he couldn't see his way to find any church, let alone stand upright at a proper altar. Ever the enabler, my earth mother joined him on this journey as their alcoholism ran roughshod over their idealism.

For as long as I can remember, my extended family floated down the river of denial whenever I played the role of white elephant spotter by pointing out their alcoholic behaviors. Instead of actually addressing my concerns, I was told they were in fact "resting" and other euphemisms designed to conceal the stone-cold reality that my extended family was pretty much passed out. It was almost as though Monty Python's "Dead Parrot" sketch was being reenacted right in front of me. My family's fantasy float trip picked up the speed of an ocean liner on July 1, 1977, my sixteenth birthday. On this date, Dad drank himself to death.

Mom died from her addictions some eleven months later. After their demise, my mother's stoic Yankee family (the ones related to the Pilgrims, Roger Williams, and other lesser-known New England religious relics) blamed Dad for killing Mom, though they soon switched to blaming me. Apparently, they assumed that as the oldest minor child I possessed this superpower that could somehow stop intergenerational alcoholism. Meanwhile, Dad's North Carolinian country club crew displayed their upper-crust sensibilities by simply pretending we didn't exist.

No wonder I became a religious satirist. With this kind of familial baggage, it's either cyanide or satire.

Thanks to the emerging research into narcissism and trauma, I can now see with clarity how I was "gaslit" and "scapegoated." For those unfamiliar with the term "gaslighting," Merriam-Webster offers this succinct definition:

> The psychological manipulation of a person usually over an extended period of time that causes the victim to question the validity of their own thoughts, perception of reality, or memories and typically leads to confusion, loss of confidence and self-esteem, uncertainty of one's emotional or mental stability, and a dependency on the perpetrator.[9]

Signs of gaslighting include lying ("You're just making this up to get attention"), discrediting ("No one would ever believe that a person with your education and social standing could be an actual abuse victim"), shifting blame ("If only you behaved better, I wouldn't have to treat you like I do"), and claiming persecution ("Your accusations are hurting my business"). If those subjected to gaslighting try to escape their situation, their tormentors will often hover around promising to do better and make the relationship work. But inevitably, they will fail to make any lasting and sustainable changes.[10]

Signs You May Be Experiencing Gaslighting (courtesy of Dr. Ramani Durvasula)

- ☐ Feeling the need to send long, explanatory emails or text messages to the gaslighter.
- ☐ Providing an "evidentiary base" for feelings (e.g., showing them old text messages).
- ☐ Recording conversations, either overtly or secretively, so you have proof of what they said.
- ☐ Being over-reliant on other people's feedback to determine how you are feeling.
- ☐ Giving long preludes before you say something.
- ☐ Feeling compelled to put all communication in writing as "proof."
- ☐ Giving in and going along to get along.[11]

And then there's gaslighting's sordid cousin, "scapegoating." If we go back to good ol' *Merriam-Webster*, they define a scapegoat as follows:

1) A goat upon whose head is symbolically placed the sins of the people after which he is sent into the wilderness in the biblical ceremony for Yom Kippur, 2) one that bears the blame for others, and 3) one that is the object of irrational hostility.[12]

Most of us take Leviticus with a Lot-sized grain of salt, but sacrificing others to ensure one's place of pride remains a key practice among those who possess strong narcissistic tendencies. As noted by Neel Burton in *Psychology Today*,

> The ego defense of displacement plays an important role in scapegoating, in which uncomfortable feelings such as anger, frustration, envy, guilt, shame, and insecurity are displaced or redirected onto another, often more vulnerable, person or group. The scapegoats—outsiders, immigrants, minorities, "deviants"—are then persecuted, enabling the scapegoaters to discharge and distract from their negative feelings, which are replaced or overtaken by a crude but consoling sense of affirmation and self-righteous indignation.[13]

Often gaslighting and scapegoating work in tandem to wreak havoc on one's psyche. Think of them as Thing 1 and Thing 2 from Dr. Seuss' *The Cat in the Hat*. Those who dare to critique their spiritual swill will be deemed crazy for pointing out that the emperor has no clothes. But should a spiritual leader decide they need to reform their ways to save public face, their critics will end up getting blamed for allowing said emperor to run around without any clothes in the first place. It's that ol' "damned if you do, damned if you don't" dealie.

Other tools in a narcissistic playbook include charm, condescension, deliberate forgetfulness, feigning intimacy, flattery, guilt-tripping, indirect insults, insinuations, minimization, rage, rationalization, and vacuous statements.[14] (Please note that the presence of one or a few of these aforementioned traits does not mean the person has extreme narcissistic qualities. Think of these behaviors as guideposts that something might be amiss, not the gospel truth, though if the number of attributes starts to multiply, odds are you're dealing with a scenario ripe for abuse.)

Discovering Narcissism

Now that I understood the basic concepts of narcissism, I realized I needed to heal from the aftereffects of being raised in a family chock-full of both alcoholic and narcissistic traits. Determined to break this cycle once and for all, in 2016 I began my foray into clinical research on the topic. Here I discovered Dr. Craig Malkin's book *Rethinking Narcissism: The Bad—and Surprising Good—About Feeling Special*. Malkin coined the term "echoism" to describe the pattern of enabling narcissists, which he derived from Ovid's *Metamorphoses*, which contains the myth of the cruel shepherd boy Narcissus and the forest nymph Echo.

In this story Echo is cursed by Juno, the Roman goddess of marriage, to be an echo chamber for others. After seeing Narcissus hunting, Echo falls passionately in love with the beautiful youth, but due to her handicap, she can only repeat the words of others. When they meet, he rejects her. In despair over her unrequited love, Echo wastes away until only her voice remains. Meanwhile, Narcissus goes to quench his thirst in a stream. When he bends over and sees his reflection, he falls in love with his own image. He lingers at the bank until he too wastes away. Echo sees his demise and joins Narcissus in his final lament.[15]

Sound familiar? Yep. In Malkin's summary of this myth, I saw myself laid out, bare butt and all. Finally, I could decipher the threads of alcoholism and narcissism woven throughout my extended family tree. In *Jesus Died for This?* I delved into my late father's pioneering work with those on the fringes, especially his research exploring why some students wanting to create a better world were drawn to Students for a Democratic Society (SDS) while others became Jesus hippies, a.k.a. Jesus People USA (JPUSA).[16] His sociological findings sound indeed godly and groundbreaking, though like others of his era, he failed to address how such hippie-led collectives could evolve into viable communities.

With the hindsight of history, Malkin's research into narcissism, and Markoe's comedic insights, I could finally see how Dad's charismatic persona and overly idealistic sermons masked signs of both alcoholism and extreme narcissism with my mother all too willing to play the role of the ever-enabling Echo. As I continued digging around my extended family tree, I realized I was surrounded by rotting familial fruit. No wonder whenever I felt particularly low, I'd yell out, "My life stinks!" The fruit from my family tree had rotted to the point where it really stank to high heaven.

In hindsight, I was saved by my spiritual director, the late Rev. Judith T. Baumer, and the charismatic community that flourished at the Manhattan-based St. Bart's Episcopal Church in the early '80s. Here I experienced a spiritual community that literally saved me. Without their support, I'm fairly certain I'd be pushing daisies by now. They connected me with the nascent recovery movement that was showing signs of promise in helping alcoholics and addicts as well as their families heal from the impacts of their addictions. Within the walls of church basements and parish halls, I learned how to avoid connecting intimately with those who exhibit signs of alcoholism and addiction.

Yet I still felt triggered when I was around people who might be sober but continued to display the same self-centered traits described in the recovery literature. Why did I continue to feel an attraction toward those with such odious personality flaws buried deep beneath their seemingly calm and charming veneer?

How could I put an end to my deep inner need to help (read "enable") people who, like my late father, presented with the potential to heal the world but instead emotionally and spiritually harmed both themselves and those around them? Even if they sobered up, why did they continue to act in the same self-centered manner as when they were drinking? What in holy hell was going on? Though I had done considerable work unpacking my familial alcoholism, my work to educate myself about narcissism so I could heal myself from the damage done by the narcissistic fruit left hanging on my family tree was just beginning.

Defining Narcissism

Overall, narcissists are characterized as having a lack of empathy for others, a need for excessive admiration, and the belief that one is unique and deserving of special treatment.[17] The mere presence of these traits does not always mean the person is a full-blown narcissist, however. For instance, when someone is stressed and emotionally depleted, they can behave temporarily in self-centered ways because they cannot see beyond their immediate needs at that moment. In addition, some who may present as self-absorbed may be suffering from an anxiety disorder, depression, or other mental health struggles, but once they stabilize and get the requisite help, they're often capable once again of displaying empathy and compassion toward others.

Dr. Ramani Durvasula notes in her book *It's Not You: Identifying and Healing from Narcissistic People*, "The reality is that narcissism is on a continuum. On the milder end, you have your superficial social-media narcissists, locked into a perpetual and emotionally stunted adolescence, which may be annoying but not necessarily harmful." On the less mild end, Durvasula observes how extreme narcissists exhibit callousness, exploitation, cruelty, vindictiveness, dominance, and even physical, sexual, psychological, or verbal violence, which may be terrifying and traumatic.[18] In this book, I am focusing on those who are at the high end of the narcissistic spectrum.

A key sign that a self-centered sort has morphed into a full-blown narcissist is when they become obsessed with themselves to the exclusion of the outside world. This shift leads them to treat other people badly in pursuit of their own desires. In terms of the spiritual leaders I've met over the decades, this translated into putting their commercial success over extending Christlike compassion.

As those who score high on the narcissism scale lack any self-reflection, they're stuck in beliefs and behaviors that prevent them from truly connecting with others. They may be experts at pretending to care by offering pointless, pithy platitudes such as "I feel your pain," "I'll pray for you," and "The universe will provide." When delivered with a well-crafted, caring veneer, they can give the illusion they possess some semblance of a compassionate soul. However, nothing you do will make them genuinely care about you. There's no there, there.

> When people show you who they are, believe them, the first time. Not the twenty-ninth time!
>
> —Maya Angelou[19]

In *The Narcissist in Your Life: Recognizing the Patterns and Learning to Break Free*, Julie Hall rightly observes how narcissists certainly aren't the only type of people who lack empathy. As she points out, it is their lack of empathy coinciding with a competitive sense of superiority, inflated entitlement, low self-awareness, and constant need for admiring attention that makes them so very toxic. They aren't just insensitive and selfish, arrogant, and devaluing, manipulative and exploitative; they are also *endlessly demanding*:

They want attention. They want approval. They want admiration. They want agreement. They want everyone around them to validate their distorted self-serving reality and continuously hold up a mirror reflecting that false reality back to them as if it were irrefutable fact. They want to mistreat others with impunity and be told they are wonderful while doing it.[20]

According to Hall, these narcissists possess an excessive need for attention, which they depend on for psycho-emotional sustenance. "Although we all have social needs, narcissists demand a level of attention beyond that of most neurotypical adults, often resorting to manipulation to get it. Narcissists figuratively suck all the oxygen out of the room."[21]

Like an addict in search of their next fix, those with extreme narcissistic tendencies need constant validation and admiration from others; this creates their narcissistic supply. Without the rest of the world to affirm their every move and give them the adoration they require, they become like a rabid raccoon. When you affirm them, they respond like Dr. Jekyll, but dare to differ with them, and their inner Mr. Hyde emerges. Just like Cinderella's carriage turned into a pumpkin when reality shattered the too-perfect fairy tale, they will transform into missional monsters the nanosecond someone stands up to their unbiblical behavior.

Whenever they perceive a threat to their ability to maintain their superficial, inflated ego, they will often exhibit a phenomenon termed "narcissistic collapse." While this phrase isn't an official psychiatric term and hasn't been extensively studied, some researchers and psychologists maintain that narcissistic collapse occurs when someone tries to expose a narcissist's carefully curated false persona. Granted, receiving criticism can be difficult for even the best of us, but narcissists will weaponize their anger against any perceived opponents, even if these critiques are offered in good faith with a genuine effort to offer correction and guidance. Weapons in their arsenal include interfering with their "enemies'" employment, cyberbullying (and encouraging their followers to do likewise), spreading misinformation to divert attention from the stench of their spiritual secretions, and serving up lawsuits.

Because narcissists are so insecure, they often feel empty and hollow—they need admiration from others to feel validated.[22] Should they fail to get enough likes, follows, and friends, they tend to either implode or explode in a desperate attempt to save their idealized, untouchable sense of self, dragging down everyone else around them in the process. But if social media stats are any sign of one's success, too many of these spiritual sorts can garner enough unhallowed hype to keep their ego overstuffed and over-satiated. Meanwhile, the rest of us remain starved for the authentic connection their words promise they will provide, but inevitably they fail to deliver the goods.

Sandy Hotchkiss, author of *Why Is It Always About You? The Seven Deadly Sins of Narcissism,* unpacks how the fantasy world of narcissists can have a seductive allure that promises to envelop others in its specialness: "Their superficial charm can be enchanting, and they often appear complicated, colorful, and exciting as they draw you into their narcissistic web."[23] No wonder being in their orbit can be such a blast; even the ugliest duckling can feel like a swan when under their spell. Those on the more egregious end of the narcissism scale take an egotist's self-centeredness one step further. It's not enough for them to simply bask in the light of their self-righteousness; they also need to ensure that their enemies languish in the dark, unseen and unheard. Furthermore, as Hotchkiss notes, "It is not uncommon, in the presence of such individuals, to feel controlled, manipulated, helpless, and angry, or on an emotional roller-coaster ride. Narcissists exude a powerful force field that is difficult to stay clear of and nearly impossible to control once you have been drawn in. They play on whatever narcissistic vulnerabilities you may have left over from earlier experiences with similar characters."[24]

Hall points out how they invert the Golden Rule, "to do unto others as you would have them do unto you," so it can suit their personal needs:

> Do unto others as I would never allow them to do unto me because I am better and more deserving, and by the way, I need you to tell me and show me that I am superior and entitled 24/7 because I am deeply afraid I'm really not, and if you don't give me what I demand right now, I'll punish the hell out of you into perpetuity.[25]

Yes, a greater percentage of men have these narcissistic traits than women, though blaming narcissism solely on the patriarchy misses the mark. I've lost track of the mean girls I've met in church and other spiritual settings. I double-dog dare you to cross a Bible-blessed spiritual sister, a wellness woo-woo publicist (especially if she's downing "mommy juice"), or an overly enlightened content creator / influencer / life coach / podcaster / whatever-it-takes-to-sell-my-spiritual-schtick shyster. In my experience, it's the quest for personal power (whether real or perceived) that defines narcissism, not patriarchal privilege. That said, the patriarchy does afford those men who possess spiritual narcissistic tendencies a ready-made platform for them to glorify their god-fearing selves in true MMA style (though as always, they're stuck in the missionary position).

How someone with narcissistic traits will display these behaviors will be contingent on their particular personality. Those who are overt in how they interact with others in public may lash out with an Old Testament–style vengeance while a more covert, quieter person will likely display passive-aggressive behaviors whereby they appear to keep the peace, all while discreetly doling out their poison to anyone they perceive to be a threat. In *Surviving Modern Yoga: Cult*

Dynamics, Charismatic Leaders, and What Survivors Can Teach Us, Matthew Remski points out how clinical psychologist Jennifer Freyd named this latter sort of table-turning DARVO—deny, attack, reverse victim, and offender: "The perpetrator or offender may Deny the behavior, Attack the individual doing the confronting, and Reverse the roles of Victim and Offender such that the perpetrator assumes the victim role and turns the true victim—or the whistle blower—into an alleged offender."[26]

In the second edition of *More Than Two: Cultivating Nonmonogamous Relationships with Kindness and Integrity,* authors Eve Rickert and Andrea Zanin note how DARVO committed by characterological abusers can be devastatingly effective because many of these folks are exceptionally good manipulators. "If they suspect someone might report on their bad behavior, they may try to 'get ahead of the story' by telling their own story of victimization first. Or they may genuinely believe themselves to be the victim, possibly because of their own sense of aggrieved entitlement, or possibly because of their partner's own reactive toxic behaviors, which they may then use as an excuse for their own," they write.[27] Unfortunately, their charisma can blind those not subjected to their abuses into believing their faux victimization stories by scapegoating those being victimized as "the problem."

Narcissism Traits Throughout History

Yes, yes, yes. I can hear it now: "We've always had self-centered sorts since the dawn of civilization, whose dastardly deeds have been recorded in the annals of history. So what?" Are we really going to do this whole "who's worst" parlor game? Marquis de Sade or Keith Raniere? King Herod or David Koresh? Aimee Semple McPherson or Joel Osteen? Hotchkiss points out how there's nothing new about narcissism, adding there have always been vain, grasping, manipulative characters who have an inflated perception of themselves and little regard for others. What she finds to be troubling about contemporary culture is the extent to which these personality flaws have received a widespread stamp of approval:

> Narcissism is not just tolerated in our day and age, it is glo-rified. Many of our leaders and the public figures we admire flaunt their narcissistic proclivities, and we can't wait to emulate their excesses. On them, outrageous behavior looks glamorous and exciting, so we give ourselves permis-sion to share in the "fun." Before we know it, the distinction between what's healthy and what isn't gets fuzzy, and "Everybody does it" becomes the justification for continu-ing down the path.[28]

Margaret Wheatley provides some much-needed historical back-ground in her book *Who Do We Choose to Be? Facing Reality, Claiming Leadership, Restoring Sanity* that helped me understand this dramatic uptick in narcissistic behaviors on display both in the church and the larger society as a whole. She unpacks the work of Sir John Glubb, who studied thirteen empires from Assyria in 859 BCE to modern Britain in 1950. In his research he documented how these empires declined in the same stages, and it always took ten genera-tions, about 250 years. Glubb defines the trajectory of civilization cycles as beginning with the age of pioneers, then following with the ages of conquest, commerce, affluence, and intellect before conclud-ing with the age of decadence.

According to Wheatley's analysis, we're in an age of decadence. Her description of this civilization cycle appears to be pulled from today's headlines:

Frivolity, aestheticism, hedonism, cynicism, pessimism, narcissism, consumerism, materialism, nihilism, fatalism, fanaticism, and other negative behaviors and attitudes suffuse the population. Politics is increasingly corrupt, life increasingly unjust. A cabal of insiders accrues wealth and power at the expense of the citizenry, fostering a fatal opposition of interests between haves and have-nots. The majority lives for bread and circuses: worships celebrities instead of divinities...throws off social and moral restraints, especially on sexuality; shirks duties but insists on entitlements.[29]

She goes on to describe how leaders in the age of decadence, acting as if they'll always be in power with unlimited resources, become hugely beneficent in offering a progressive society to all: human rights, social justice, gender equality, education, and health care benefits all surge ahead during this last stage of societal collapse as leaders create the welfare state.[30] Inevitably, this benefits bubble will expand until it becomes so unstable and unsustainable that it bursts spectacularly, thus transforming what was once a land of plenty into *Lord of the Flies*.

As history has amply proven, such unstable periods of global dysregulation would also seem ripe for slick spiritualists who score on the highest end of the narcissism scale to dominate our sociopolitical discourse. Upon further examination, we see these efforts becoming commercialized and commodified by those self-appointed thought leaders who promise they will lead a movement to co-create a new way of being that attracts those seeking to "live your best life now," "become a new kind of Christian," "harness the law of attraction," and other sappy spiritual slogans. In the end, these manipulators chose to promote their platform instead.

On the cultural level, narcissism can be seen in a loss of human values—in a lack of concern for the environment, for the quality of life, for one's fellow human beings. A society that sacrifices the natural environment for profit and power betrays its insensitivity to human needs. The proliferation of material things becomes the measure of progress in living, and man is pitted against woman, worker against employer, individual against community. When wealth occupies a higher position than wisdom, when notoriety is admired more than dignity, when success is more important than self-respect, the culture itself overvalues "image" and must be regarded as narcissistic.

—Alexander Lowen, *Narcissism: Denial of the True Self*[31]

While one can find charismatic charlatans in the mix since the dawn of civilization, we need to be careful not to play mock-historian by interpreting historical eras through a contemporary lens. For starters, the term "narcissist" is a relatively recent addition to the public lexicon. Hence, while the Marquis de Sade may have been just as narcissistic as NXIVM founder Keith Raniere via moves like branding women, the language used to describe Sade's debauchery would not have included contemporary psychological terms.

The late Christopher Lasch's book *The Culture of Narcissism: American Life in an Age of Diminishing Expectations*, first published in 1978, points to the rise of self-centered behaviors in the United States. Lasch lashed (wonder how often he got that joke hurled at him) against the swells of self-centeredness that marked the '70s Me Generation. This era was followed by the "greed is good" glitz that defined the '80s. Ironically, this period not-so-co-incidentally marked the era of megachurches, the New Age movement, the Religious Right, and a few too many televangelist sex scandals.

Everybody—the right, the left, the believers, the unbelievers—is aggrieved that our society is not just on shaky ground but in really serious trouble. There are literally hundreds of reasons that explain that common opinion. One of the clues to our depravity and our sickness is our celebrities. We have the most goof-ola bunch of celebrities in social and cultural history.

—Steve Allen[32]

In their book *The Narcissism Epidemic: The Age of Entitlement*, authors Jean M. Twenge and W. Keith Campbell note how those religious and volunteer organizations that aligned themselves with individualistic values have thrived while those that have not have often withered.[33] Their research pointed to the reality that genuine church growth is contingent on valuing the contributions made by each member of the community in lieu of elevating a charismatic charlatan, who will inevitably fleece the flock.

Unfortunately, their prophetic words failed to halt the greedy gravy train that continued in both the church and secular cultures until the stock market crash of 2008. Since then we've been in a spiritual free-for-all, searching for signs of meaning with self-proclaimed healers popping up whack-a-mole style to sell us their version of the ultimate spiritual salve that will somehow save us all. A review of their "prophetic" products makes me think they were more self-serving than spiritual.

Not surprisingly, publishers picked up on these trends. Many books began to speak to the rise of narcissistic traits within the U.S. sociopolitical culture and how to deal with "difficult" church leaders well before President Donald J. Trump graced the national political stage. For this reason, I would like to shift this conversation away from "Trumpvangelicalism" and focus instead on analyzing a portion of society that continues to elevate narcissists: specifically, the Christian church and its outgrowths.

Stay tuned to see what happens when someone not only thinks, "I am my own God," but decides to put this unbiblical belief into practice.

2
Prey Not Pray: Unpacking the Unspiritual Dimensions of Narcissism

Now that I've outlined the basic tenets of narcissism, what are the added dimensions of spiritual narcissism that give missional malignants that "Well isn't that special?" *SNL*-Church-Lady veneer?

Dana Carvey played this bespectacled Bible b*tch for laughs; when the Church Lady pondered, "Could it be Satan?" we all were in on the joke. At the same time, there's nothing funny about those "Christian healers" who consider spiritual narcissists to be agents of Satan, even though I agree the carnage created by spiritual succubi is downright hellish. Despite a recent resurgence in some incel settings that suggest elements of the '80s era Satanic Panic,[1] methinks these alarmists need to rethink their theology and their psychology. I have yet to find any credible, peer-reviewed work proving that Satan is playing matchmaker by pairing curious Christians with spiritual narcissists. Let's leave such disreputable dogma behind along with the mullets, New Coke, and other '80s junk.

So, as I dig into the particular proclivities of predatory pastors and their ilk in this chapter, rest assured that I will not be calling upon any powers of exorcism. Though spiritual narcissists use the beliefs of their victims against them, they hardly need any special spectral power to do so—just their faith that they are the most important person in the room, if not the planet.

© NakedPastor

Spotting Signs of Spiritual Narcissism

At its core, spiritual narcissism is a psychological pattern where individuals exploit spiritual practices and beliefs to reinforce their inflated sense of self-importance.[2] These ungodly gurus cherry-pick and twist religious texts, ecclesiastical titles, slogans, and other signifiers of their particular brand of faith to justify their behaviors. Even though they may mouth the appropriate words needed to sound sincere, they do not live out those principles. They may bless those who follow them, but in the end, they will prioritize their commercial success over extending Christlike compassion or Buddhist blessings.

Any sign in the universe will be misinterpreted as ontological proof that they're the lead singer in the Spiritual Supremes. They'll not only brag about their number one holy hits but insist that all their followers must sing along to their leader's lyrics. But watch out if anyone tries to change the channel or encourages other voices to sing their own songs. Worse, see what happens when anyone dares to compose their own creations, thus depriving their leaders of claiming all the credit for this co-creation. These religious renegades will quickly find themselves subjected to "thoughts and prayers" encouraging them to repent of their wayward ways. Come back into the fold and follow, follow, follow.

Those on the end of the narcissistic spectrum can go so far as to believe they are their own god or goddess. In their self-proclaimed role as the ultimate Almighty, they justify utilizing their authority to control those under their spell, even at the expense of crossing ethical and legal boundaries. Examine the claims any spiritual leader makes about their work. Do they offer to help guide seekers along their journey, or do they promise they can heal you from all that ails you? Remember that a true spiritual guide will offer support, but they will not play miracle worker.

Strolling Along the Spiritual Bypass

Psychologist, psychotherapist, and author John Welwood coined the term "spiritual bypassing" in 1984 to describe a common tendency he discovered among aspiring Western mystics to use spiritual ideas and practices to avoid dealing with their emotional unfinished business.[3] Watch them flaunt their faith on Facebook, which they crosspost to Instagram, TikTok, X, LinkedIn, Substack, Rumble, Truth Social, Pinterest, Bluesky, YouTube, Threads, WhatsApp, Telegram, Signal, Reddit, and any other online platforms I might have missed. Then there's the unpastoral pillow talk on, say, Christian Mingle, eHarmony, Ashley Madison, and Tinder that should give any sane spiritual soul considerable concern.

Their practices are not paths toward actual enlightenment but badges of honor they display like pastoral peacocks. All their social media feeds are chock-full of pictures and videos documenting their perfect practices, not to mention audio and text filled with spiritual-ese: Anointed, Awakened, Blessed, Energetic Healer, Gaia Goddess, Higher Consciousness, Inner Enlightenment, Karuṇā Care, Lightworker, Manifest, Reiki-inspired Religion, Saved, Washed in the Blood of the Lamb, or any other pat phrase designating them as more spiritually evolved than us mere mortals. They'll career along the spiritual bypass like they're trying to win the Indy 500, all the while uttering meaningless phrases like, "My 'thoughts and prayers' are with you," "It's God's will," or "The universe will provide." They don't have any time to stop and offer any actual concrete help or even a sincere hug that at least acknowledges the problem at hand.

While true transcendence centers on the sense of connection and similarity between self and others, a spiritual narcissist is driven by a need to be separate from and better than their fellow humans.[4] Not only are they more evolved than others, with a super-special connection to the deity of their choosing, but they belittle those who do not follow their specific practices and beliefs. Time to cue up that ol' classic from the Austin Lounge Lizards, "Jesus Loves Me (But He Can't Stand You)."[5] Their charming persona and enticing promises convince their disciples they are members of a special tribe of chosen people through which blessings will flow to them. But—and this is a big but—you only get your blessings if you buy, buy, then buy some more into their message.

© *The Wittenburg Door*[6]

Here the term "buy" is used both metaphorically and literally. For one to be accepted as a member of a particular theological tribe run by a super-duper spiritual narcissist, one must buy into their message while also buying their products. Just pony up the cash for their latest book, subscriber-only Substack, branded fast-fashion clothing, and whatever other swill they're selling. As long as you keep paying the piper, maybe, just maybe, you can ride along. But if you forget to fork over your faith and funds, they'll ride off into the sunset without you.

Cashing in for Christ or Chakras

The Christian Industrial Complex and multinational mindful movements headed by shamanic superstars encourage this dynamic as they benefit from the money and publicity generated by self-appointed spiritual masters. These institutions have a sordid history of elevating select gurus to positions of power. When questioned about their support for unbiblical blowhards, these faith-based fixtures express contempt, calling their critics "unawakened," "un-evolved," "unenlightened," and other soulless slams. This long-standing inability to put into practice the Greatest Commandment to "love thy neighbor as thyself" continues to advance the self-interests of elites in power, keeping their devoted fans captive to their whims. These self-anointed sages are aided and abetted in their quest by their faithful followers along with those who stand to profit from these pseudo-prophets' platforms, such as book publishers, denominations, conference and festival organizers, speaker bureaus, brand managers, literary agents, and personal publicists, in conjunction with a compliant media all too willing to hype up this unholiness if the price is right.

If a spiritual sleaze lands a publisher willing to fork over the requisite cash to buy their place of pride on best seller lists, they have now entered the "too big to fail" category. Some may choose to donate some of their ill-gotten gains to their favorite charity cause under the guise of "doing good." Since these charities need these funds in order to survive, even when they learn of abuses committed by their key benefactor(s), they know to remain silent lest they lose their faith-based funding.

Should a spiritual superstar's dastardly deeds get exposed, their newfound celebrity status has now granted them admission into an inner circle filled with best-selling Christian and secular exploiters. This group of malevolent missionaries bands together by quoting and endorsing each other's works, further cementing each of them as invaluable experts spouting a Teflon-like theology that supposedly can't be touched. Just follow the money; then you can see what they truly worship.

Here are a few examples. An aging progressive spiritual surfer speaking at a faux-progressive/affirming church in Portland, Oregon, called me a "plant" when I questioned his conservative funding streams. I smiled Southern-style and said, "No," grateful I could keep my calm while asking him the kind of questions I knew had to be asked despite our mutual discomfort. The audience smiled in tacit agreement with him, while looking at me as though I had invaded their holy sanctuary after eating a bean and cheese burrito bowl.[7]

Then there's the spiritual surfer's sidekick, a firebrand who once told an acquaintance of mine, "It doesn't matter what I believe. It matters what sells." Continuing this "woe is me" meme from manipulators, an emergent thought leader whose work has grown spiritually stale bemoaned to a colleague, "I hate when people critique me, as it impacts my book sales." Now factor in all the multilevel marketing (MLM) moves within the woo-woo wellness, mindless meditation, and sacred sexuality for sale that clogged up my social media feeds when I began researching this book. You get the gist. All me and no we.

Let's face it: spiritual narcissists pull moves that would make the Baby Jesus soil his diaper. Dunno about you, but I lack bandwidth right now for such a dump.

Top Ten Signs Your Church Might Be Led by a Spiritual Narcissist[8]

10. Always emerges as the victorious warrior during theological smackdowns.

9. Their missional motto: "I said it. I believe it. That settles it."

8. In lieu of church bingo, they play the shame game.

7. Their tattooed theology is in tatters.

6. Favors Bible beatings over blessings.

5. The church sign may say "Welcome" but their greeters are the Frozen Chosen.

4. Always leaving on their private jet plane.

3. Claims their book sales are doing better than the Bible.

2. Feels up and then fleeces their flock.

1. More ostentatious than Osteen.

The Rise of Narcissism in the Church and Other Spiritual Settings

According to research data, between 0.5% and 5% of people in the U.S. may have Narcissistic Personality Disorder (NPD), the official diagnosis given by therapists to those whose behaviors fit the definition for clinical narcissism.[9] For some time, anecdotal surveys have placed clergy among the top professions that attract those whose narcissistic traits have risen to this level.[10] Along those lines, in *Surviving Modern Yoga*, Matthew Remski reports that researchers estimate that there are five thousand high-demand groups in the United States alone engaging between ten and twenty million people. (Typically the "high-demand" and "high-control" refer to groups where the leaders exert control over their followers' lives, demanding complete commitment and adherence to the group's beliefs and practices.) Remski suggests that perhaps the large-scale rise of such toxic groups led by spiritual narcissists should be viewed as a public health issue.[11]

However, the limited surveys exploring narcissistic traits in pastors appear to be flawed in their methodology, with no comprehensive studies examining the prevalence of narcissism among leaders of high-demand churches and other spiritual settings.[12] More research is needed on this topic, analyses that goes beyond citing Google as gospel and scrolling through social media in search of the latest #NarcTok nonsense. I'm advocating for a return to academic research, replete with a qualified peer-review process, proper sourcing, fact-checking, and other basic Journalism 101 skills. Aim for actual, not AI generated.

But who will fund this research? After all, those at the top of the faith-based food chain either ignore the need for an investigation or, worse, they thwart anything that might threaten their current social and financial status. Perhaps the academies devoted to church and ministry, especially if they receive funding from major donors such as Lilly Endowment Inc. or the Templeton Foundation, are by nature the last places where this type of in-depth research might begin.

Also, it's harder to see a problem worth researching when most spiritual leaders who display behaviors associated with extreme spiritual narcissists tend not to fit the clinical definition for the diagnosis of NPD. According to the clinical definition of NPD as it stands, if a narcissistic person isn't suffering from their symptoms to the point where their life becomes significantly impaired, they don't have an actual mental health diagnosis. Hence, using a diagnosis of NPD to screen for extreme narcissism among these spiritual superstars is a dead end.

Spiritual narcissists who rise to positions of leadership tend to possess enough charm that they're exalted as visionary thought leaders by those who only focus on their glowing press releases—and this is hardly impairing, but enabling and emboldening. Ironically, the very traits that render these leaders unable to form real human connections can catapult them into the media spotlight to be lauded as the next big thing destined to "save Christianity" (I kinda thought that was Jesus's job, but I digress), "manifest a global transformational movement," or other sappy slogan that might entice a potential pilgrim to take a bite. No matter how delectable the dish is, consuming this faith food will most likely induce a spiritual stomachache, or worse . . . much worse.

The role of narcissism within Christian circles didn't draw national attention until the emergence of Trumpvangelicals and the countering #churchtoo movement, which grew out of the grassroots #metoo movement and focuses on abuses by Christian leaders. The stories of survivors point to the preponderance of toxic behaviors among both progressive pastoral posers and caped Calvinist crusaders. The past few years have also seen a dramatic spike in stories of abuses in other spiritual settings. Upon closer examination we can see the threads of narcissism woven into the fiber of both our religious and secular institutions. Therefore, focusing on one individual's personality flaws, no matter who happens to be the latest pantsless pastor, the trendiest tattooed theologian replete with designer sneakers, or the sleaziest sexual healer, misses the mark. These individuals only represent the symptom, not the root cause behind these narcissistic energies. The nanosecond a bestselling big shot leaves the stage by either hook or crook, a newer and shinier unholy hotshot arrives on the scene to take their place.

Brad Sargent's (a.k.a. Futurist Guy's) research points to how these self-serving narcissistic leaders are adept at leveraging the hopes and fears, desires and ideals, grievances, and values of potential adherents. "They understand their audience and capitalize on such intangibles to create a magnetic connection that draws people into their trap," he observes.[13] Their overuse of stock community-building phrases like, "a rising tide lifts all boats," "we're all in this together," and "go team" can give the impression they're spearheading a genuine community designed to welcome others in true Billy Graham fashion: "just as I am."

Imbued with the spirit of self-righteousness, these charismatic charlatans utilize their charm and confidence to exploit their audience through tactics like *love bombing*, a form of psychological and emotional abuse that involves a person going above and beyond for you in an effort to manipulate you into a relationship with them.[14] Like an overeager suitor, they will flatter and praise you to bits, often showering you with unexpected (and often unwanted) gifts and other signs of affection while projecting the promise of a magical future together, should you choose to follow them. Finally, we can see, hear, and perhaps even touch someone who spouts slogans that mirror the same dreams and ideals we've been visualizing. In this enthralled state we can be tempted to join in their crusade even though their words might sound just a bit too good to be true.

In *Near Enemies of the Truth: Avoid the Pitfalls of the Spiritual Life*, Christopher D. Wallis references how modern Buddhism uses phrases such as "near enemies." This term refers to "states that appear to be similar to the desired quality but actually undermine it."[15] (In comparison, "far enemies" refers to those qualities that represent the exact opposite of what we wish to manifest; they are thus much easier to avoid). When we want so desperately to believe a mirage is magic, we can easily tune out our inner voice and praise the narcissist's puffery without realizing we're in the presence of a near enemy. Whenever we hear phrases geared to soothe us into a state of bliss (also known as complicit silence), we need to pull out a navigational map and read the waters. If we're willing to open our eyes and our minds, it often becomes crystal clear that this particular spiritual sort is sailing solo to god or goddess knows where—though they will bring along a deckhand or two to do the dishes and the dirty work.

The ABCs of AREs

While we're on the subject of doing the dirty work, Beth Schwartz, Ph.D., RN, offers this definition of Adverse Religious Experiences (AREs):

> Adverse Religious Experiences (AREs) are internalized, often prolonged encounters within religious systems, teachings, or relationships that result in psychological, spiritual, emotional, physical, sexual, financial, and relational harm—especially for women. These experiences may involve shame-based messages, rigid doctrines, gendered oppression, spiritual bypassing, and conditional belonging. AREs disrupt a woman's sense of self, impair her decision-making autonomy, and contribute to a loss of bodily trust, sexual agency, and personal sovereignty.
>
> Rooted in women's stories, AREs often manifest subtly— normalized or spiritualized within religious cultures—yet they deeply affect core areas of life. Financially, women may be coerced into dependence or pressured into tithing or unpaid labor. Sexually, AREs can promote purity ideologies that lead to fear, dysfunction, or disconnection from one's own body. Relationally, AREs may enforce silence, submission, or isolation, especially in the context of abuse. Over time, these experiences can fracture identity and health— until the woman begins a process of recognizing harm, restoring inner connection, and reclaiming her self-worth.[16]

John Pavlovitz, pastor, activist, and author, offers these observations as to why AREs persist despite a never-ending stream of books, podcasts, and other forms of media offering ample resources on how to reimagine a new kind of Christianity, live your best life now, and other branding B.S.:

> Because modern church culture is both consumer-driven and competitive and results are desired quickly, many communities are built backward, in that they usually begin with a person (or a personality) around whom a staff is assembled. A building is found or built, services are designed, and supporting ministries are created—all to serve the vision of the minister. In this context, the church's ability to draw people to their services depends on personality cults and worship styles, thus elevating the small number of people involved.[17]

In Karl and Laura Forehand's experiences helping people heal from AREs through their work with The Desert Sanctuary, they developed the belief that pastors and church planters never set out to hurt people. "Their founding principles and goals were most likely to help people, but the survival of the organization eventually took precedence and cast a shadow over any effort to truly deal with people's trauma. Leaders eventually use their fear against them to motivate them to pursue corporate goals," Karl opines.[18]

This dynamic helps explain why over time some pastors transform from helping to harming those under their care. Other spiritual leaders, who envision themselves as God's representatives here on earth, chose to situate themselves on a pious pedestal at the start of their ministry in anticipation of the expected adoration they feel they so righteously deserve.

Trauma-Informed Theology

Now, I'm not advocating that we all run out in search of an ever-elusive nirvana where we can finally dwell in paradise. Dave Johnson and Jeff VanVonderen, co-authors of *The Subtle Power of Spiritual Abuse*, remind us that a perfect family or church where people never get hurt simply doesn't exist, but they take care to differentiate between an abusive and a non-abusive system. They observe, "While hurtful behaviors might happen in both, it is not permissible to talk about problems, hurts and abuses in the abusive system. Hence, there is no healing and restoration after the wound has occurred, and the victim is made to feel at fault for questioning or pointing out the problem."[19] As this book focuses on spiritual narcissism and not religious trauma and abuse, I will not delve deeply into these topics. However, I will leave you with a brief overview of the impact spiritual narcissists can have on those they choose to target.

The term Religious Trauma Syndrome (RTS) was coined in 2011 by psychologist Marlene Winell to describe the negative impacts a patient experiences from prolonged exposure to a high-control spiritual group. Indoctrination with false beliefs, customs, and rituals advanced by high-control blessed bullies forces followers to not only take a particular spiritual path but also to share their personal life secrets, financial gains, and social networks with the group, along with engaging in victim-blaming toward anyone critical of said leaders and their inner circle. The clinical features of this syndrome include weak critical thinking skills, difficulty in making decisions, decreased sense of self-worth, difficulty building strong relationships, being unfamiliar with mainstream culture, a sense of isolation or struggling with fitting in and belonging (fish-out-of-water feeling), nightmares, sleeping issues, eating issues, sexual dysfunction, anxiety, a sense of grief, guilt, fear, and loneliness.[20]

In *Bully Pulpit: Confronting the Problem of Spiritual Abuse in the Church*, Michael J. Kruger outlines the key aspects inherent to spiritually abusive scenarios. While he addresses pastoral abuse, these characteristics can apply to anyone in spiritual leadership:

❑ Abusers typically have what appears to be a fruitful, gospel-centered ministry with a track record of success.

❑ Abuse often happens for years, leaving a long "debris field" of broken relationships before it finally catches up with the abuser.

❑ Abuse involves domineering, bullying behavior, leaving the abused in genuine fear, especially if the abuse involves threats of church discipline.

❑ Reports of abuse rarely lead to accountability, as friends defend the abuser and the board (often made up of people much younger in age or experience) provides alternative explanations.

❑ The victims of the abuse are typically forced out and charged as troublemakers who are attacking a faithful pastor just doing his job.[21]

Wade Mullen draws comparisons between the behaviors of many abusers and a stage play: "There are front-stage behaviors and back-stage behaviors, and the two are often quite different. What happens on the stage is designed to appeal to the audience, hiding what happens behind the curtain." In his book *Something's Not Right: Decoding the Hidden Tactics of Abuse—and Freeing Yourself from Its Power*, Mullen delineates three types of environments that are designed to keep abusive backstage behavior from being discovered:

Secrets

Five types of secrets—dark, strategic, inside, entrusted, and free—help to keep abusers in power. Abusers will often hide dark secrets (like abusive behavior) behind another, more legitimate kind of secret.

Sacred Roles

Environments where certain roles are viewed as special or sacred can be ripe for abuse, especially if those roles are necessary for the community to function ("keystone" roles).

Inner Circle

Environments where those in leadership are closely connected in multiple ways (e.g., families or friends) can become abusive as those in power try to protect themselves instead of the vulnerable.[22]

Connie Baker, author of *Traumatized by Religious Abuse: Courage, Hope and Freedom for Survivors,* observes how by definition, "any abuse consists of some type of power differential—where one person has more power than the other and hurts the other person with that power." She adds,

> [In spiritual settings,] this power can be perceived or real and can be held by one religious person or a small or large group of religious people, or it can be implicit in the rules of the whole religious organization. The abusive person or institution has some sort of power that the abused person does not have and uses that power (usually leveraging religious ideas or the idea of God) to manipulate, control, hurt, exploit, suppress, silence, or weaken the other person.[23]

According to Baker, signs of a spiritually abusive situation include:

- A strong emphasis on spiritual, familial, and organizational authority
- The use of fear, guilt, shame, and superstition as motivators
- An emphasis on being a "special" or "unique" group along with promoting an "us versus them" mentality

- The substitution of members' previous addiction with religious addiction
- A demand for unquestioning loyalty
- A strong adherence to and reliance on patriarchal structure
- Members who often feel off-balance, confused, manipulated, and exhausted
- Extreme ideas around sexuality—either demanding extreme repression or combining sexuality and spirituality without acknowledging the power differential that can lead to abuse
- The use of coded language that's required to gain entry into the group along with the use of rigid black-and-white religious ideas and language to gain the compliance of members
- The use of denial (by members and leadership) to protect against confusing and destructive reality
- Engulfment into the group by requiring members to devote considerable service, time, energy, and money[24]

Not every group that exhibits a few of these signs would be considered riddled with abuse. Gatherings that rally around, say, a sports team, an entertainment icon, or a social cause, as well as fraternal organizations and alumni clubs, often employ coded language, dances, and other markers as signs of team loyalty and camaraderie. By all means, love the Lambeau Leap, flash the friendship bracelets, and clap your hands when your local charity hits its fundraising goal.

Just watch your wallet and wits so that you're not extending yourself beyond your financial means or participating in a group that's more cult-like than truly connective. History has shown that once a spiritual leader with extreme narcissistic tendencies gets a seeker to commit to their self-proclaimed "caring" community, this new convert quickly becomes indoctrinated in the rules they must follow in order to remain as one of the "chosen ones," though some choose to exit at this juncture, as they aren't interested in divine dancing now that the spiritual steps have changed.

Others stay, as they believe that the ultimate communal good, coupled with any personal benefits promised by their newfound spiritual community, outweighs any discomfort endured when the spiritual master dares to discipline their flock. Those vulnerable due to life-changing circumstances (e.g., rejection by a church, relocation, failed relationships, loss of employment, a recent death, or a serious illness) are especially susceptible to the love bombing tactics narcissistic leaders of high-control systems employ to ensure their faithful followers remain compliant and loyal to their whims.

Over time, love bombing turns into trauma bonding, a mental state described as a hormonal and psychological attachment caused by repeated abuse with just enough "loving" gestures and promises of a better tomorrow (also called "future-faking") sprinkled in to entice devotees to remain faithful.[25] Signs of trauma bonding include blaming yourself or innocent others for the perpetrator's abusive behavior, avoiding any behaviors that might set the abuser off, becoming preoccupied with and anticipating the abuser's needs and wants, and having a detailed accounting of the abuser's schedule and habits.[26]

According to researchers, the trauma bonding that occurs in abusive relationships may be at least partly due to hormones outside of our control. In *Healing from Toxic Relationships: 10 Essential Steps to Recover from Gaslighting, Narcissism, and Emotional Abuse*, Stephanie Moulton offers a short biology lesson that explains this phenomenon:

> Your autonomic nervous system—or the part of your nervous system that controls your involuntary movements—is made up of the sympathetic nervous system (SNS) and the parasympathetic nervous system (PNS). In simplest terms,

SNS gets your body ready to weather stressful events and the PNS returns your body to its normal state afterward. When you have a fight or experience conflict, your SNS activates. Your adrenal glands send the hormone adrenaline into your body, triggering a cascade of other hormones to put your body on high alert—your heart rate and blood pressure increase, your breathing becomes more rapid, and your senses sharpen.[27]

The research behind and biology of trauma bonding is still emerging. What is known is that those experiencing these sensations will typically have a fight, flight, freeze, or fawn response. Those who fight back (like me) or flee by getting the heck out of there tend to be the ones who get gaslighted and scapegoated for blowing the buzz. Conversely, those who freeze find themselves abused under the pretense that their silence equals complicity, while those engaging in fawning like behavior often receive public praise for their undying devotion.

Slowly, I began to grasp the reasons behind my visceral reactions to the seemingly over-the-top responses I got when satirizing American Christianity for *The Wittenburg Door*. The ongoing and sustained attacks by those who went Ba'al-istic whenever I satirized their work would trigger me as they brought up memories of prior familial incidents too numerous to count. With each attack, I'd find myself re-traumatized: with the current cycle of abuse being swirled into my past traumas until my emotions de-evolved into a stinky spiritual stew not fit for human consumption. But when I was fortunate enough to land in a setting filled with care and compassion, I could achieve a state of inner peace, even if only for a moment.

Here I need to distinguish between trauma and abuse. Both terms convey the sense that one has been affected negatively. But too often

they are used inter-
changeably. Think of
abuse as actions taken
by those seeking power
over us, to our detri-
ment, whereas trauma
is our body's response
to the unresolved
impact of these actions.
Extended contact with
a person who displays

"Just remember guys: you are doing this for God, not for me!"
© NakedPastor

extreme signs of spiritual narcissism can lead easily to first abuse, then
the long-lasting impacts of trauma.

Evangelizing the Enablers

Trauma doesn't exist in a vacuum but requires three sets of players:
abuser(s), enablers, and watchers. Durvasula describes enablers as
"the people in your midst who keep cutting the narcissistic person
slack: families or religious communities who may shame you for
not forgiving the narcissist, a society at large that tells you that you
can't "quit" your relationship or even call out bad behavior, people
who minimize what you are experiencing or fall into tired explanations like 'You aren't perfect, either.'"[28] In his book *When Narcissism Comes to Church: Healing Your Community from Emotional
and Spiritual Abuse,* author and licensed therapist Chuck DeGroat
describes how churches (and I'd add any spiritual community) are
particularly susceptible to a dynamic called "collective narcissism."
He defines this as "a phenomenon in which the charismatic leader/
follower relationship is understood as a given."[29] In this scenario,
zealots behave similarly to the throngs of disciples following Brian
in *Monty Python's Life of Brian* who disregard his pleas not to

follow him or anyone else but instead to think for themselves. Their sycophantic responses of praise and adoration include shushing the lone voice that tries to stand apart from the prevailing groupthink.

In *The Facebook Narcissist: How to Identify and Protect Yourself and Your Loved Ones*, Lena Derhally introduces the Collective Narcissism Scale (CNS), a tool she notes can help identify if a given group is experiencing this phenomenon. This scale ranks a number of statements from 1 to 6, with 1 meaning "totally disagree" and 6 meaning "totally agree." The statements are as follows:

- I wish other groups would quickly recognize the authority of my group.
- My group deserves special treatment.
- I will never be satisfied until my group gets the recognition it deserves.
- I insist on my group getting the respect that is due to it. It really makes me angry when others criticize my group.
- If my group had a major say in the world, the world would be a much better place.
- I get upset when people do not notice the achievements of my group.
- Not many people seem to fully understand the importance of my group.[30]

The leader of a group who scores high on the CNS will praise de-individualization by encouraging those in the group to act as a collective: "Just free your mind. Then follow, follow, follow. Obey, Obey, Obey." Once a follower's brain is blown, their empty shell of a body can be remodeled and remade into whatever shape the narcissistic leader envisions a true disciple should resemble.

Collective narcissism can perhaps be evidenced most plainly by the fury their followers hurl at those who dare question the teachings of their latest and most faithful master. Challenge the spiritual status quo, and you're now considered to be unsaved or unenlightened and damned to hell (or h-e-double-toothpicks if one is Southern Baptist). The true believers, who are often drawn to charismatic leaders in a quest to heal themselves from abusive and traumatic wounds, now take delight in abusing those their newfound spiritual leader designates as the enemy.

Derhally, a licensed psychotherapist certified in Imago Relationship Therapy, unpacks how the concept of the Wicked Witch of the West and her henchmen applies to those who enable narcissists: "'Flying monkeys' is a pop psychology term used to describe the people the narcissist uses to do their dirty work . . . Once the narcissist finds a suitable target, they will use the flying monkeys to gossip, spread rumors, relay messages, and torment their newfound target. The monkeys are easily manipulated by the narcissist and will believe the lies without question. Sometimes, flying monkeys are also narcissists."[31]

Overt enablers can be easy to spot. They're the ones who elevate abusers by endorsing their books, inviting them to speak at conferences and other promotional opportunities, donating money and expertise that prop up this person, and attacking and dismissing those who raise legitimate concerns, all in a bid to keep abusers in positions of power. At first glance these enablers often present themselves as professional organizers and movement makers, but they too can lack boundaries and perpetuate guru gushing. It's extremely commonplace.

Then there's the more covert ways that uber volunteers can find themselves in an enabling pattern. They have a habit of ever-present hovering in the background, all too ready to keep the Christian circus or spiritual show running, going so far as to put the concerns of the community and its leaders ahead of their personal needs and wants.

Over time they find themselves experiencing cognitive dissonance, the feeling that their belief system contradicts the purportedly valid feelings and thoughts they keep experiencing. No matter how often they try to ignore the warning signals, they keep popping up, similar to the Whos that kept trying to get Horton's attention in Dr. Seuss's *Horton Hears a Who.*

Even when someone is aware they're in an unhealthy scenario, they often experience what's called the "sunk cost effect" (also known as the "sunk cost fallacy"). Moulton describes how this dynamic occurs when someone continues to invest their time and talents into a relationship even though the situation is not in their best interests: "You don't want to feel you 'wasted' that time, so you're less likely to leave or end the relationship," she opines.[32]

When we investigate the sunk cost fallacy on the corporate level, we can see why whole denominations or associations are often unwilling to hold their leaders accountable for their behaviors, especially if the abuser has risen to the level of spiritual superstar, where their unbiblical buzz generates both media mentions and money. As demonstrated by the onslaught of lawsuits facing the Catholic Church, we can't ignore the reality that *if* an institutional body admits they knew of abuses and stayed silent, not only are they enablers, but they subject themselves to legal action that could put them out of business. And let's face it, way too many institutional churches care way more about business than the Bible.

If we return to the three sets of players introduced at the start of this section, we will see that most people in a religious or spiritual community fall into the third category of "watcher." They might not take part in or enable the abuse, but when allegations start to arise, they choose to remain silent and subservient to their glorious godly guru so they can still be part of the cool kids club.

Megan Benninger of Baptist Accountability's Guide for How to Enable an Abuser[33]

- Public apologies are expected to be accepted at face value before sustained actions toward repentance/reconciliation are observed.
- Members/followers are inclined to give the benefit of the doubt to the accused rather than the victim. People feel so sorry for the accused and all that the exposure is putting him through. Hardly anyone mentions what the victim must be feeling, what toll it must be taking on them.
- Members/followers repeat ad nauseam that no church/ organization is perfect.
- Victim blaming. Members/followers continually point out that there are two sides to every story. They point out flaws and mistakes the victim made and imply it is equivalent to the abuses committed against them. This is also called sin-leveling in spiritual abuse terminology.
- If the victim continues to be upset or continues to speak out about problems, they are seen as problematic. Their mental health is called into question. ("They have trauma" and "she probably is borderline" are just two comments I've seen so far.)
- Members/followers chastise the people criticizing the offender by saying they are overreacting, not being forgiving, and threatening the unity of the church/organization.
- Members/followers insist that their situation is different, not as bad as others, and insist their leaders are well-intentioned.
- Members/followers believe their church/organization will do the right thing starting now—no matter how strong the patterns of the past might be.

Continuing the Spiritual Spin Cycle

Throughout his book DeGroat points to how "in recent years we've witnessed too many instances of charismatic Christian leaders gaining a massive following, both within the church and on social media, only to be exposed as manipulative, abusive, and dictatorial."[34] Over time it's to be expected that the spiritual spotlight shining on today's theologian du jour will begin to lose its luster. But even if a given spiritual leader gets removed from their community, the lingering psychological impact of their behaviors will continue to have toxic reverberations that impact the group until it becomes an evangelical-istic epidemic. It can stink. Here's a few odiferous ways the stench of spiritual narcissism continues to linger well after the offender leaves the room: emotional manipulation and turmoil; erosion of trust and authenticity; disruption of healing and growth; strained relationships and isolation; and diminished self-worth and empowerment.

No wonder groups headed by such sorts tend to dissipate following revelations of abuse. Even if the leader's physical presence is no longer felt, the nose knows something still stinks. No matter how hard those left behind try sterilizing this stench, some scents will linger forever.

Closed for sightseeing

© Becky Garrison

The Long-Term Impacts of Spiritual Subjugation

Daniel Shaw, LCSW, has emerged as a pioneer in researching the impact of spiritual narcissism on individuals, a topic informed by his own experience in a high-control group. In *Traumatic Narcissism: Relational Systems of Subjugation*, he emphasizes how pathological narcissism causes relational trauma, yet he "encountered little theorization about how predominantly over-inflated narcissistic people traumatize significant others—by attacking the other's subjectivity."[35] In layman's terms, this means basically destroying the core of one's personhood.

Shaw summarizes his formulation of the psychology of the traumatizing narcissist thusly:

> In response to developmental trauma, specifically including cumulative experiences of extreme shame and humiliation, from parents and the wider environment, the nascent traumatizing narcissist grows up and finds a solution for his shameful feelings of powerlessness, or impotence: he develops a manic delusion of omnipotence. A central aspect of this delusion is shamelessness—the refusal to acknowledge or recognize as appropriate any form of shame relating to one's being and behavior. He or she views himself or herself as perfectly infallible, and infinitely entitled, and therefore in no need of growth or change.[36]

He then describes how these grandiose, overinflated narcissists seek hegemony for their subjectivity by weakening and suppressing the subjectivity of others:

> They control and exploit followers by seductively dangling carrots—which in this context would be what purportedly could be achieved by becoming a follower—such as

success, fulfillment, wealth, or enlightenment. Along with the carrots comes the relentless use of sticks, such as humiliating character assassination and threats of expulsion, meant to persuade the followers that their own subjectivity is inadequate and corrupt compared to the leader's, and therefore in need of extensive correction that only the group and its leader can provide.[37]

Following are a few tools Shaw discovered that can be found in the traumatizing narcissist's toolbox:

Purification of Ego. The follower's deficiencies are grouped under the umbrella of "the ego," the "monkey mind," or a similar idea using different words, which is regarded as a harmful appendage or blockage of the true self, and must therefore be "purified" by the leader for the follower to reach her potential.

Only Perfection Is Good Enough. By demanding perfection, the leader makes it impossible for the follower to fully succeed at anything, including devotion, and therefore it is impossible for the follower to avoid the leader's abusive criticism.

Incessant Urgency. The more successful and powerful a particular leader becomes, the greater the risk of public exposure, and, therefore, the more urgent and hysterical the culture becomes.

Violation of Boundaries as a Norm. As followers discover that no effort they make is ever good enough to earn the leader's full recognition or to make them exempt from the leader's destructive attacks, they become more and more desperate to please the leader, becoming willing to let down their own boundaries and to violate the boundaries of others at the leader's behest.

Inner Deviance Must Be Eradicated. Ultimately, followers act on the belief that only the leader's thoughts and feelings matter and have validity, and the follower must exist only to serve the leader's aims. The follower actively seeks to negate any aspect of his own subjectivity that the leader might disapprove of.

Defend the Leader No Matter What. By now a follower has often become so ensconced within the group that they can-not see these patterns (at least for the time being). But should they start to feel signs that something is amiss, Shaw's findings can help them identify the root cause for their unease. Also, knowing these signs can greatly aid spiritual seekers in determining when a very welcoming community might be per-haps a bit too cultish for one to make any genuine connections.[38]

© *The Wittenburg Door*[39]

Not My Church

Before we proceed, don't think I don't see you progressive Jesus follow-ers and a/theistic academics sitting off in the corner like some smug teenager watching their enemies get called out for their evangelical excesses. You might want to re-examine that whole "log in your eye" dealie before calling out your neighbor's itty-bitty speck. Just sayin'.

True, denominational systems can serve as a check and balance against unbiblical behavior, but this hierarchical structure creates a system ripe for elevating those at the top as exalted thought leaders worthy of worship. Too often institutional systems produce ample opportunities for bishop butt kissing, pew posing, and other moves that point to celebrations of power, not prophecy. If an ordained progressive clergy or lay person achieves some degree of media exposure to the point where they are awarded a spot at the Christian celebrity carnival, they're now giving their dying denomination some much-needed media exposure and hopefully congregants and cash. Hence, should this person engage in abusive behaviors that come to light, then their particular denomination will be faced with a unique dilemma: How should they respond when the very person they're promoting as their spiritual savior proves to be not your typical run-of-the-sinner but a serial abuser? It happens.

Even when mechanisms are put in place to address problems of clergy-related abuses, the response so far seems to be offering "thoughts and prayers" but limited practical assistance to prevent further #churchtoo abuses. Take, for example, the revelation of multiple sex scandals impacting the Church of England that led the Archbishop of Canterbury to resign in 2024.[40] True, they set up a safeguarding system to address issues of clergy abuse though their responses to date still seem to favor priests in power over supporting survivors in their recovery from church related abuses. So at least they have a formal albeit imperfect system in place compared to their counterparts in the United States, who continue to keep a stiff upper lip when asked about particular pastoral peccadilloes, especially those involving bishops. Purple over people, I suppose.

No wonder I can no longer call myself an Episcopalian in good faith. I didn't leave the institutional Episcopal Church. It left me.

Quiz: Are You a Spiritual Narcissist?

For those spiritual leaders who are questioning if they are indeed blessed or full of B.S., here's a survey that can help you figure out the extent to which you might be a spiritual narcissist.[41]

1. You're the self-appointed leader of a spiritual community with a public mission to manifest a new heaven that transcends our earthly dimensions. Despite your godliness, yet another cult documentary[42] has been released detailing abuses within your midst. Do you . . .

    A. Close down the community, allow law enforcement to do a thorough investigation, and compensate the survivors of said abuses.

    B. Discretely give those perpetrators accused of abuse(s) enough money so they will simply fade away.

    C. Hire a crisis PR rep to go gonzo on any journalist who dares to ask questions.

2. During a hurricane in your city, your megachurch (formerly a basketball arena) is one of the few places that remained dry. You've been asked by the city if those flooded out of their homes can camp out in your church until the water subsides and they can return to their homes. How do you respond?

    A. Welcome everyone in with no questions asked.

    B. Allow people to stay at your church but then bill FEMA for the cost of cleaning up the place (even though the cleaning bill is less than what it costs to tidy up your mega mansion).

    C. Refuse to allow anyone in because they will muddy up your sanctuary, thus making it too unclean for worship services. However, if you get subjected to undue media scrutiny, you might relent and do a performative fundraising drive.

3. Back in your evangelical megachurch preaching days, you elevated an internationally known "family values" leader to elder status and accepted millions from them. Their donations were used in large part to launch your international bestselling author/speaker career whereby you marketed yourself as a kinder/gentler progressive evangelical religious rock star who was affirming toward the LGBT community. When asked about these donations from someone who actively campaigns against LGBT equality, your response is . . .

    A. OMG, I am so, so, so sorry for my prior work with this person. I will donate any money they gave to my ministries to organizations that work to help LGBT kids damaged by their public proclamations. Also, I will issue a full apology on my website and work with LGBT groups to do better in the future.

    B. Oops. Didn't mean to do that. My bad. Let me write about how to care for gay and lesbian people in my next book. I'll deal with bisexuals and transgenders later, I promise.

    C. Are you a plant? I mean, just who paid you to come here and ruin my ministry?

4. You are penning a book about human sexuality from a hipster Christian perspective. Given how many books on this topic have been penned by both secular and religious scholars, your publisher tells you to come up with a unique way to market your manuscript to the missional masses. Do you . . .

    A. Research the living daylights out of this topic until you have an actual body of work that builds on prior study of human sexuality in addition to shedding new light on the subject.

    B. Write a book that dumps on the fundamental/evangelical church's approach to S-E-X while ignoring your own mainline denomination's failings on this hot-button topic.

    C. Launch a campaign to promote your book whereby you have purity rings melted down into a vagina sculpture that you gift to your favorite feminist icon as part of a glitzy, exclusive lily-white women's conference.

5. You scored an invitation to the annual National Prayer Breakfast. What do you do?

    A. Politely decline, stating you cannot support organizations that do not promote church/state separation.

    B. Accept the invitation so that you can do "social good" by networking with the various international groups gathered there.

    C. Use this invite as a PR marketing tool to promote yourself as one of the DC prayerful power players.

6. As the head of a seemingly liberal mainline denomination, you've been asked to address multiple allegations of inappropriate behavior by leaders under your charge. How do you respond?

    A. Launch a full-scale investigation and let the chips fall where they may.

    B. Apologize for any harm that may have been caused, and then allow any alleged abusers to resign with a full pension and other perks.

    C. Scold those who make any claims of this nature to "be nice." Then issue a statement declaring that at least your leaders didn't engage in acts of extreme child sexual abuse like those Southern Baptist perverts or sex-crazed Catholics.

7. At the start of your bestselling book tour, a major natural disaster such as a hurricane, a tornado, or a flood hits your home city that directly impacts some members of your congregation and the larger community in ways that will forever change their lives. Do you . . .

    A. Put people over promotion. If you can't be there in person, you arrange for backup pastoral support to tend to your community's needs while using your book tour as a fundraising vehicle to help those in need.

    B. Open each book event with a moment of "thoughts and prayers" for those affected by the disasters, and then continue with your program.

C. Stay calm and carry on while making no mention of this disaster lest you kill the mood and thus limit your book sales.

8. You've been invited to speak at a spiritual conference or festival that will feature an author/speaker with a very well-documented history of multiple abuses. After survivors of this person's abuse and victim advocates confront you by presenting indisputable evidence, how do you respond?

A. You apologize to those victimized and inform the conference organizers that you cannot take part in any event that gives a known abuser a platform to promote their products.

B. You tell those critiquing your participation in this event that you promise to be a prophetic witness against #churchtoo abuses, though in the end, you drink beer with the theobros instead.

C. You block all those who criticized your participation while posting to social media praiseworthy pieces from the event including pics with you and the aforementioned author/speaker.

9. A national LGBT organization created a video profiling a caring minister welcoming a lesbian couple and their young child. When they ask to run this video as a paid advertisement on your popular progressive Christian media platform, what do you do?

A. Post the advertisement and promote it repeatedly with multiple blasts across all your social media channels.

B. Accept the ad but then bury it by posting it late Friday afternoon right before a holiday weekend and just let it die a quiet death.

C. Reject the ad on the grounds that it will offend your conservative funders. Then block anyone on social media who dares to critique your progressive street cred.

10. You are a white, straight, cisgender male who is asked to speak on an issue that impacts a demographic that doesn't describe you. How do you respond?

   A. Gently refuse the offer and recommend other voices who are part of this demographic, adding that they are the most qualified to speak on this topic.

   B. Accept the invite, but be sure to point out how many ethnic minorities, women, gays, and lesbians are part of your network. In this equation bisexual and transgender individuals aren't included.

   C. Go on the show and blast anyone who calls you racist or sexist by pointing out how many "friends" you have who are Black or female. Conveniently ignore any anti-LGBT accusations because God Almighty told you not to associate with such degenerates.

Score

Give yourself 1 point for every A answer, 2 points for every B answer, and 3 points for every C answer.

10-11 total: You're a selfless saint. If there were more people like you in the world, there would be no need for religious satirists. Keep doing the work, and I hope those with ears to hear can tune in.

12-21 total: You're like most divine dolts, just trying to get by without being too big of a spiritual scumbag, though the blandness in your work might explain why your numbers keep dwindling. Simply put, you talk a nice talk, but your actions don't match your message. Been there. Done that. Next.

22-30 total: Yay! You win the prize for the spiritual narcissist of the year. But of course, you knew that already.

3
Identifying the Types of Spiritual Narcissists

Now that I've unpacked the basic tenets of spiritual narcissism, what are some telltale signs that one has encountered a leader who has the characteristics attributed to an extreme spiritual narcissist? The answer to this question may not be as simple as it first appears. Despite the fact that signs of narcissism are everywhere in American spirituality, as evidenced by the preponderance of catchphrases like "Jesus said it. I believe it. That settles it," "The Episcopal Church Welcomes You," and "Embrace your inner goddess," spiritual narcissists don't fit into neat and tidy, easily identifiable clinical definitions. After all, with well over forty-five thousand denominations[1] constituting the world of Christendom (not to mention boatloads of Buddhists and other spiritual practices), there's a wide range of personalities claiming to speak on behalf of the god or goddess of their choosing. That said, in this chapter I'm going to attempt to satirically summarize the different types of narcissists, both for the sake of making such sordid spiritual souls easier to identify out in the wild and, in disparaging them, to give them less power over the rest of us.

Given the variety of religious experiences, to paraphrase philosopher and psychologist William James, exactly how spiritual leaders display the signs of extreme narcissism will differ depending on their given personality type. As a refresher, in the introduction to this book I broke down the different types of spiritual narcissists into the most common six categories defined by those clinical therapists and academics whose work I've quoted in this book: exhibitionist, grandiose, royal, victim, seductive, communal, and malignant.

Also, when reviewing these categories, be mindful that these spiritual narcissists can fall into more than one category. For example, in *The New Science of Narcissism*, W. Keith Campbell explains how grandiose and vulnerable narcissism are two related but separate expressions of this personality disorder. He observes that while both forms of narcissism share a core of disagreeableness, self-importance, and a sense of entitlement, they differ a great deal in terms of what added traits they blend with that core. "With grandiose narcissism, you see confidence, boldness, and self-esteem, but with vulnerable narcissism, you see low confidence, anxiety, and low self-esteem," he notes.[2]

Consider the latest progressive poser du jour, who might be a grandiose exhibitionist and display malignant tendencies in their mistreatment of those who disagree with their biblical branding, but also all the while they claim to be persecuted for their quasi-radical stands on contemporary hot-button social issues. Communal types who claim they are creating a collective cooperative here on earth can easily morph into a spiritual showman should their work bear fruit; conversely, they may display signs of victimhood if they feel their "worthy" projects never come to fruition. Prosperity gospel preachers are exhibitionists in their stage performances while promoting a cozy Christian message as they run their church like a corporate Christian. Then there's the sexual shaman who overpromises that they can manifest sex magick, but once they're unmasked as a malignant molester, they'll claim they're being targeted for their otherworldly beliefs.

Therefore, I advise you to use these categories more as guides than definitive descriptors of the narcissists in your midst. What all of them have in common is that in the end, it's an unsacred sh*t show focused solely on them as the unreligious ringleader. For those seeking a detailed and in-depth academic analysis of the different types of spiritual narcissists, check out Brad Sargent's *Futurist Field Guides*.[3]

As for the elaborated descriptions of the different narcissistic categories that follow, feel free to play amateur detective by writing in the margins your own descriptors and reflections on the narcissists you encounter in your own pilgrimage. Given the nascent research into spiritual narcissism, we have much to discover together.

Finally, as you embark on this journey, please be sure to bring along your sense of humor and play. I find the more I can counter someone's spiritual swagger by exposing them as yet another emperor who's not wearing clothes, the less I allow them to impact my soul and spirit. Sometimes cliches ring true: laughter is indeed my best medicine for such missional madness.

Blinded by My Light: Exhibitionist Narcissists

Description: These self-appointed unhallowed hucksters are marketed by the Christian Industrial Complex and its secular counterpart, the monied mindfulness movement. This multi-media publishing empire, unique to the American culture, produces celebrities who focus on building and maintaining their personal platforms over serving as bona fide spiritual leaders.

Media depictions of these leaders tend to highlight the exhibitionist narcissist's over-the-top antics, thus giving a false impression that all spiritual narcissists are super-duper showstoppers. In fact, exhibitionist narcissists are the rarest breed, with most others adopting a more genteel veneer so they can more easily appear to be both superior and saintly.

Other narcissists will often display hostility toward the exhibitionist narcissist's over-the-top pastoral preening, but their angry outbursts often mask their jealousy over not being in the spotlight themselves.

Identifying Markers:

- Overt narcissist: They are number one (at least in their mind) as they showboat their superior spirituality as the "Chosen One."
- Theme songs: "Personal Jesus" (Depeche Mode) followed by repeated rounds of "Applause" (Lady Gaga).

- ❑ Humblebragging about their narcissistic traits as they showcase their shadow side for all to see.
- ❑ Charisma and charm that draw in both crowds and cash.
- ❑ Like any addict, they can go ballistic if they don't get their daily fix of admiration, adulation, and attention.
- ❑ Takes great pride in their work as a spiritual influencer/content creator by uploading their devotionals online 24/7 to their multiple social media channels, while displaying a complete lack of shame or even common sense when hawking their wares.
- ❑ Highlights select sacred texts to justify their personal awakening and faith-based fantasies of power.
- ❑ Only endorses and recommends works by their fellow bestselling buds.
- ❑ Often spotted taking credit for others' work.
- ❑ Known for name-dropping and hogging the spiritual spotlight.
- ❑ When giving a public speech, they cannot distinguish between playful jokes and bullying—can dish it out but not take it.
- ❑ Decked out in designer gear tailored to their branded persona, whether that be a holy hippie, religious rock star, megachurch millionaire, biblically button-downed, mindful mommy, faith fairy, conscious cultural appropriator, and so on. Selected branded merch available for sale.
- ❑ Founded a church plant, nonprofit, or other collective for the purpose of self-promotion, not the creation of an actual community, which they will leave for another similar setting should too many concerns get raised about their unbiblical behavior.

Where to Find:

- ❑ Headlining conferences, festivals, and other events where they can be the main attraction

- The *New York Times* bestseller lists the week their latest book launches, though their not-so-pious PR tends to die down once their publisher stops paying their publicist for placement
- Private online platforms managed by their brand manager, publicist, or a-bit-too-devoted fan, with special benefits available to paid subscribers
- Headlining the latest, greatest church or other spiritual entity
- Media outlets that produce PR puffery, especially cable talk shows and podcasts
- As per the riders attached to their public performances, they must fly first class, be allotted five-star hotel treatment, and be granted godly goodie requirements for their green rooms
- Lives behind the velvet rope in the VIP suite

How to Safely Approach: Unless you're part of their inner circle, do not attempt to communicate with them in person unless you're willing to fork over considerable devotional dollars for meet-and-greets, video greetings, Zoom counseling sessions, and other one-on-one encounters. Often they are surrounded by gatekeepers who tend to their every personal whim while keeping the fanatics away (armed bodyguards with Secret Service–style earpieces optional).

Should you choose to play spiritual spectator, be aware of how these swindlers can draw you in with their scummy shtick. The slicker their spiritual sh*t, the sleazier they get. To avoid getting bitten beyond belief, it's best to view them as a performance artist. No matter how blissed and blessed the buzz from their B.S. may feel, do not under any circumstances start fantasizing about how this person could become your best bud. Nor should you presume that their disciples will ever coalesce into an actual community. Instead, view any time spent with an exhibitionist narcissist and their crew as an adult version of Spring Break, a communal happening where their faithful fans come together to yell, "You Go, Guru!" Just remember that binge believing is remarkably similar to binge drinking in its long-term impact on your internal organs and personal relationships. Protect your energy and be willing to walk away when the buzz starts to sting.

Preaching to the Prosperous: Grandiose Narcissists

Description: These gilded prosperity gospel preachers possess an unrealistic sense of superiority: a view that they are blessed by an almighty power and are therefore better than others. While these over-the-top televangelist types lend themselves to religious ridicule, signs of grandiose narcissism are present in less obvious ways among those, for example, who follow *The Secret* and other positive-thinking movements. This promised wealth and other blessings will come to those who literally buy into the "if you can believe it, you can achieve it" line of thinking: they agree to pay in order to play and pray.

Identifying Markers:

- Overt narcissist: They're richer and better than you.
- Theme songs: "You're So Vain" (Carly Simon) or, for the more prosperity gospel–minded, "Plastic Jesus" (Billy Idol).
- Always seen in public with an ungodly grin and the hair that praises Jesus.
- Brags about their money, power, and prestige while equating any growth of their bank accounts and promotional platform to proof they're in alignment with the Almighty.
- Spiritualizes their power plays by claiming they're following god or goddess while demonizing those who question their spiritual authority.

- ❏ Inflates their sense of cosmic importance by giving themselves elevated titles such as High Priestess, Prophet, and Starseeker. These must be used by those who choose to follow them, or else.
- ❏ Preaches to their disciples that for the right price, they can be their own god or goddess (though in their mind, they are the one true God).
- ❏ Prefers to plagiarize, as they think copyrights are for cowards.
- ❏ Faith-based flasher decked out in gold and glitter in the hope that this armor will guard against their deep-seated feelings of inadequacy and insecurity.
- ❏ Seen auditioning for HBO's *The Righteous Gemstones*, thinking it was a reality TV show.
- ❏ Funnels their followers' donations into their personal piggy bank or LLC (Swiss bank and offshore accounts optional).
- ❏ Sings their version of TikTok Theology while surrounded by a heavenly choir of paid angels.
- ❏ Justifies the exorbitant prices for their services by claiming their spiritual energy represents "sacred currency" that must be paid before followers can access what they claim is the only portal to the divine, with some going so far as to believe they are the actual reincarnation of a superior being.

Where to Find:

- ❏ TBN
- ❏ Daystar
- ❏ An Oprah and Osteen orgy
- ❏ Private Lear jets
- ❏ Living in McMansions
- ❏ Serving as a divine masculine/divine feminine leader in Twin Flame–type communities

- Word of Faith, New Thought, or any other movement promising their followers big bucks and holy healing
- Setting up shop as a soul-preneur to hawk their wares, with VIP add-ons for those enlightened enough to access their "frequency"
- The latest streaming documentary detailing godly glitz
- Always on the top rung of their latest MLM scheme

How to Safely Approach: Just like in Vegas, always keep your eye on your wallet. Their primary targets are those in vulnerable life situations, so avoid them at all costs if you're going through a rough spot. They will play on your insecurities with the false promise that you will be amply rewarded if you contribute to their spiritual shams. Should you feel tempted to buy into their blinged-out blessings, call a friend, meditate, or whatever else you need to do to get yourself out of your funk. Seek professional help if you cannot stop your compulsive desire to enter into their MLM madness.

The Corporate Christian: Royal Narcissists

Description: Some churches and religious institutions are run similarly to a corporation: their finances and programming are controlled by a select group of capitalist Christians. Like their secular corporate counterparts, the leaders of these institutions maintain control via their social rank and wealth. These represent the most elusive of all narcissists, as one needs the proper pedigree for entry into their inner enclave. Also, in true WASP fashion, they eschew media coverage, preferring their names be mentioned in the press only upon major life markers: birth (and other product launches), marriage (and similar corporate mergers), and death (obituary in the *New York Times* preferred).

Identifying Markers:

- Covert narcissist: they never flash their wealth in public, preferring to exercise their full financial control behind closed doors.
- Theme songs: "My Way" (Frank Sinatra) or "Jesus Loves Me (But He Can't Stand You)" (The Austin Lounge Lizards).
- Thinks *The Official Preppy Handbook* is a reference manual.
- Their family name is plastered all over the church property.
- These blue bloods blend blessings, the Bible, and business to describe the ministry's mission using corporate-speak.
- Well-mannered and manicured.

- Giving those they deem unworthy the spiritual silent treatment.
- Often spotted clutching their pearls as they imbue themselves with hubris-infused holy water.
- Claims abject poverty whenever they have to dip into their savings, 401(K), or trust fund.
- Serves the homeless on Thanksgiving, Christmas, and Easter while decked out in their Junior League garb.
- More debutante than devotional, they wish they could be Mrs. Betty Bowers, America's Best Christian.[4]
- Possesses a sphincter-like spirituality.

Where to Find:

- Wall Street (the best believers have seats both on the vestry at a top-tier church and on the NY Stock Exchange)
- Climbing up the corporate ladder instead of carrying the cross
- Corporate boardroom (can be difficult to discern the difference between the office of the CEO of a Fortune 500 company and a rector leading a Corporate Church™ or a guru meditating in his multimillion-dollar megamansion)
- Country clubs that serve golf and gin
- Ivy League colleges and Episcopal divinity schools
- Godly gated communities
- The very best faith-based funding streams (especially Lilly Endowment Inc. and the John Templeton Foundation)
- The Social Register
- LinkedIn (though all social media accounts are managed by their personal assistant)

How to Safely Approach: Forget it. Unless you possess enough funds and social clout to enter their exclusive Christian country club or gated gurudom, you'll be left out in the cold.

The Persecuted Poser: Victim Narcissists

Description: These sad sacks pride themselves on winning the gold medal in the persecution Olympics. No matter what hardships you may have endured, they've experienced far worse. While many initially feel sympathy for them given the legitimate nature of their constant complaints, pull back their mask of religious persecution, and underneath you'll find a self-centered and self-righteous soul.[5]

Identifying Markers:

- Covert narcissist: Their narcissistic traits can be so well hidden behind their story of woe that they will initially present as a genuine victim.
- Theme songs: "Loser" (Beck) or "One" (Harry Nilsson).
- Draws people to them via their carefully crafted passive-aggressive pity party that conveys a ring of truth while masking their self-righteous rubbish.
- Blames others for their problems without taking responsibility for any role they may have played in their current predicament.
- Turns any conversation around so the focus shifts to them.
- Becomes extremely defensive or even paranoid when others dare to differ or they are given healthy, constructive criticism.
- Disguises their extreme self-doubt and neuroticism as supreme humility.

- Displays sad puppy dog eyes when begging for money or attention, only to then lash out and bite those who extend a hand whenever any help provided isn't "enough." Conversely, any gifts or aid they may offer will come with major strings attached.
- Continually active on social media in their quest for solidarity around their suffering, all the while threatening to leave a given online platform when they don't get the praise and puffery they feel they so rightly deserve.
- Often self-medicates with alcohol and drugs.

Where to Find:

- Trying to launch yet another nonprofit, church plant, or other community without first analyzing why their prior ventures failed to produce long-lasting results
- Partisan cable news shows that align with their claims of faux persecution
- Protest rallies and other gatherings where they can commiserate with their fellow persecuted peons
- Living in their parent's basement or couch surfing with friends
- Wandering around like a nomad, going from place to place in search of people who can meet their never-ending cycle of "needs"
- Soliciting money 24/7 on GoFundMe to cover their current "crisis"
- Volunteering, volunteering, volunteering, all the while complaining about how "underappreciated" they are for their valiant efforts

How to Safely Approach: Keep your boundaries intact and your tone neutral. If you feel called to help, set a limit on how much of your time, money, and talents you can provide, and then stick to it. Do not engage with their drama. A victim narcissist will suck all the positive energy out of the room. They will bring you down, not lift you up. Think Debbie Downer on steroids. If your time with them proves to be more draining than delightful, consider limiting future interactions. Snooze or even unfollow/unfriend on social media to preserve your mental health if necessary. Those with very strong empathic souls need to be mindful not to cross that line where a genuine concern for a fellow human being's welfare and a sincere desire to help devolve into becoming a devotional doormat (a.k.a. co-dependent).

Comfy Christianity:
Seductive Narcissists

Description: These Christian leaders focus primarily on the curation of a refuge from the world, one designed to allow their followers to feel good about themselves rather than addressing the actual needs of those they claim to serve. Those who become members of this exclusive church membership buy into the leader's mentality that they are in fact spiritually superior rather than putting the Greatest Commandment into practice.

Identifying Markers:

- Covert and very, very, very cozy narcissist.
- Theme songs: "Macarena" (Los del Río) or, for the more megachurch minds, "Jesus of Suburbia" (Green Day).
- Often dressed in light pastel colors replete with spiritually infused rose-tinted glasses and permanent markings on their wrist from wearing their branded WWJD? or friendship bracelets a bit too tightly.
- Oozes toxic positivity and kills with kindness through sugar-coated sayings like "Bless your heart," "The Power of You," and "God works in mysterious ways."
- Claims spiritual authority to justify their self-serving moves, all the while smiling 24/7 as they hawk their version of happy-happy-joy-joy swag.

- ❏ Filled to the brim with Gwyneth Paltrow's Goop garbage.[6]
- ❏ More materialistic than meditative while masking their manipulation via phrases like, "This is your divine purpose," "This is a sign that the universe wants us to connect," or "God/Goddess brought you here for a very special purpose."
- ❏ Love bombs believers to bits with promises that they can join an exclusive community with special secret teachings, blissful blessings, and holy healings, but they never deliver.
- ❏ Really, really, really into Reiki, despite their "treatments" not producing any tangible results.
- ❏ When asked about any hot-button social issue, they'll claim silence is golden.
- ❏ Offers personalized mentorship for those with plenty of money.

Where to Find:

- ❏ Wheaton College
- ❏ Christian Mingle
- ❏ High-end retreat centers
- ❏ Megachurches with padded chairs and Christian-sponsored coffee shops
- ❏ Hawking their branded® MLM wellness woo-woo
- ❏ Upscale Christian and spiritual bookstores
- ❏ Spiritual Facebook groups, Instagram, and TikTok where they post Hallmark-y memes
- ❏ Church hopping and temple trading. Similar to bar hopping, comfy Christians and self-satisfied spiritual seekers will go out searching for whatever godly gathering that day can furnish them with the best songs, social activities, and snacks.

How to Safely Approach: If you're having a bad belief day, their products can give you a temporary high, similar to the experience of consuming a Starbucks Java Chip Frappuccino® with extra whipped cream. But while their offerings may feel really good going down, be mindful of any adverse aftereffects that will inevitably come up. Leave at the first sign of a spiritual stomachache or a case of the religious runs.

Kinder, Gentler, More Compassionate Communities: Communal Narcissists

Description: As more Christians walk away from egregious examples of commercialized Christianity, some self-appointed progressive leaders seek to package a form of faith that on the surface appears to be affirming and inclusive. In a similar fashion, Western gurus repackage Eastern teachings into an easily digestible program that promises enlightenment, a new way of being, and other goodness goo.

While most narcissists focus on themselves, communal narcissists base their identity on what they do for others. Words used to describe their acts they perform in the name of the public good include helpful, trustworthy, charitable, kind, good, virtuous, selfless, kindhearted, and generous. But while they talk constantly about their open and compassionate hearts that seek to embrace the collective good, they can't seem to get off their spiritual sofas.

Communal narcissistic-minded leaders claim to welcome all, pointing to their movement as "leaderless," with everyone having an equal voice. They advertise themselves as non-teachers, curators, and other terms that point to a more equalitarian model of being in community. But do the math, and it's clear these groups are run primarily by cisgender white men with the occasional token person of color, woman, or LGBT person included to give the illusion of diversity. These "missional males" maintain their power through their pastoral platforms, which they've showed via their publications, podcasts, and public appearances.

Identifying Markers:

- ❏ Covert narcissist: seldom seen, though their presence is always felt.
- ❏ Theme songs: "We Are the World" (USA for Africa) or "Losing My Religion" (REM).
- ❏ Dons branded clothing and other gear designed to virtue signal they're "liberal" and "inclusive" even though they only hang around those who act and think exactly like them.
- ❏ Talks like a Dharma so they can avoid being psychologically vulnerable while responding to any criticism involving their ministry with plastic platitudes such as, "Let's all be nice," "This is a negativity-free zone," and "Om, Ohm, Aum (repeat ad nauseum)."
- ❏ Pontificates about how little money they need to survive without taking into account how much intern (read: free) labor is required so they can live comfortably while giving the illusion they live like a beggar monk.
- ❏ Declares others cannot understand their mission because they have yet to achieve the proper state of "high vibrational awareness."
- ❏ Adopts the mantra of a "servant leader" but continues to seek out the spotlight under the guise of "servant leadership." They might pass around the mic to give the illusion that all have a voice, though in the end, they have the final say.
- ❏ Tendency to drop the communal facade and morph into an exhibitionist narcissist once they achieve fame and power.
- ❏ Pillar of the community replete with humanitarian awards proving just how "good" they are and repeated posts about their charitable deeds on the latest post-progressive social media platform,

with a proclivity to offer "thoughts and prayers" while providing limited, if any, concrete assistance.

❑ Refuses to engage in any conversations pertaining to abuses committed within their circles on the grounds that these attacks represent "witch hunts," though they will inevitably side with the abusers.

Where to Find:

❑ Fair-trade coffee shops
❑ eHarmony
❑ Alternative Christian and sacred spirituality festivals
❑ Zegg forums, talking circles, and Non-Violent Communication (NVC) trainings (drums and peace pipe optional but preferred)
❑ Beer 'n' hymns
❑ Dumpster diving
❑ Theology pubs
❑ Intentional communities filled with white folx living in multi-racial neighborhoods
❑ Mainline seminaries and a few select quasi-progressive evangelical colleges
❑ Conversations about how to co-create community (provided, of course, that they can market a book about this quasi-collective experience)

How to Safely Approach: Difficult to spot at first, as their honorable deeds often outweigh their sacrilegious conduct. But don't be fooled by their faithful facade: these feel-good efforts often have little to no actual impact on those they claim to serve. If their mission resonates with your soul, think twice before forking over your funds and your faith. Do you see any actual fruit of their labor? In almost all cases, any money raised will be spent on projects that continue to generate positive vibes, not on anything that might realistically produce any transformative change. Be mindful should you find yourself giving, giving, and giving to the point where you're giving your all and receiving nothing in return sans the occasional "thanks for your kind support" form letter.

Might Makes Right: Malignant Narcissists

Description: Any form of spiritual narcissism can rise to the level of malignancy, whether it begins as exhibitionist, grandiose, royal, seductive, victim, or communal. Think of malignants as narcissists on steroids. These spiritual sharks are among the deadliest of all the narcissists, given their use of violent language and other forms of emotional and psychological abuse. Left unchecked, this abuse will escalate to physical violence, sexual impropriety, and other unethical and even criminal behaviors. Wherever they go, they leave un-Christlike carnage and guru garbage in their wake. No matter what storms a malignant narcissist may generate, they remain very firmly convinced of their righteousness and will claim amnesia whenever abuses emerge. As such, they believe they are acting within the letter of the law, even if the law dares to differ.

There is some overlap between malignant narcissism, sociopathy, and psychopathy, as all three are characterized by an inflated sense of self-importance and a strong need for admiration, as well as engaging in actions that are both harmful and unethical, if not illegal. A key difference is that a malignant narcissist will justify the "righteousness" of their actions, as they feel they've done nothing wrong. In comparison, a sociopath or psychopath will knowingly engage in harmful actions without caring one whit how their actions impact others. While there are some differences between sociopaths and psychopaths, overall these terms describe a set of traits that fall under the larger umbrella of antisocial personality disorder (ASPD), though more research needs to be done on this topic.

As I noted at the beginning of this book, I refuse to play armchair analyst but leave the actual mental health diagnoses of NPD and ASPD to licensed professionals. Hence, I will simply label those who display the traits that follow as malignant narcissists, and recommend seeking professional counsel if you find yourself dealing with someone whom you feel fits the criteria for sociopathy or psychopathy.

Identifying Markers:

- Overt narcissist: Most display missional mania, though some are the quiet, saintlike souls that no one expects.
- Theme songs: "Blurred Lines" (Robin Thicke with Pharrell Williams & T.I.) or "American Jesus" (Bad Religion).
- Throws down their theological smack online to prove they're biblical badasses or spiritual swashbucklers with the intent to destroy and defame their perceived enemies.
- Responds to *any* critique of their ministry with threats of legal action, smear campaigns, and other nefarious nonsense. Encourages their followers to engage in devotional doxing by publicly posting their targets' confidential information online, often obtained via fraudulent means.
- Preoccupied with fantasies of power and prestige as they weaponize their spiritual authority and teachings using tools like guilt, fear, and shame to force their flock to obey as they prey.
- Publicly righteous, privately wretched.
- At the slightest sign of discomfort, they will turn into a rageaholic and fling their faith-based feces to create chaos in place of community.

- ❑ Love bombs their most vulnerable targets into total compliance only to then brag about those they abuse as signs of their dominance.
- ❑ Isolates and controls their disciples through "spiritual discernment" by claiming only they can determine who is safe and who is dangerous.
- ❑ Retaliates against their perceived enemies by serving up revenge as a dish served cold.
- ❑ Posts pics of themselves with puppies to give the illusion they're cute and cuddly.
- ❑ Reads *Fifty Shades of Gray* for relationship tips.
- ❑ If caught with their pants down, will diffuse any questionable (and possibly criminal) behavior on the grounds they're suffering from "sexual addiction" or have been "tempted" into sin by a Jezebel spirit, or pretend they have a diagnosis like autism that renders them unable to read social cues.
- ❑ Often rejects social norms but more resembles an a-hole than an actual anarchist. Might don T-shirts, hats, bumper stickers, jewelry, and placards emblazoned with offensive and violent imagery on both the extreme left and right that goes against the message espoused by the Prince of Peace they profess to follow.
- ❑ Hateful in their holiness as they practice a remorseless religion (no guilt, no glory) that espouses a schadenfreude form of spirituality. If spotted with blood on their hands, it ain't the blood of Jesus, though they'll claim they're imitating Christ's suffering.

Where to Find:

- ❑ Starring in one of the latest cult documentaries streaming on Netflix, Hulu, or HBO Max
- ❑ Any setting desperate for someone who can save their dying ministry, spiritual community, or prophetic nonprofit

- Stronger Men–sorts of conferences (with an occasional female biblical badass 'n' unholy hoedown thrown in for good measure)
- Ashley Madison
- The White House and Congress
- Leading protests that push zealots to engage in acts of violence
- The subject of survivors' accountings of their #churchtoo abuses
- Any partisan cable TV show or social media platform that hasn't kicked them off for unbiblical behavior
- A court-ordered psychological evaluation where they receive an official diagnosis of NPD
- Prison

How to Safely Approach: Use the same care and caution when approaching someone with malignant traits that you'd deploy for interactions with other venomous vermin such as poisonous spiders, stingrays, and snake oil salesmen. Do. Not. Actively. Engage. For these spiritual vampires to thrive, they need to feed on the blood of others.

Keep reciting that ol' recovery mantra: KISS (Keep It Simple, Stupid). Let your tone and topics of conversation be as neutral as possible. If you must speak to them about anything more substantial than the weather, seek out qualified professionals to assist you in establishing a clear plan for how to interact with this person. Do not confront someone with malignant traits in a public setting without bringing along adequate support. They'll just DARVO the night away, leaving you alone on the dance floor like you're the loser trying to do the theological tango all by yourself. If possible, bring along a buddy so that at least you can have an actual dancing partner.

Document any interactions with them should you need further evidence of their misdeeds. A trauma-informed therapist with training in religious trauma can help you untangle the un-Christian carnage and other spiritual slop they leave behind in their wake. Find a victim advocate if you wish to seek justice for any wrongs committed.

96 Gaslighting for God

Gray Rocking Your Way to Goodness

For those times when you find yourself in the presence of egregious energies, a technique I've found to be particularly helpful in dealing with these types of folks is "gray rocking." This technique creates an invisible boundary when dealing with those whose energies tend to set you off. Think of this person as a gray rock: Boring. Bland. Blah. Instead of making an effort to connect with them, make yourself as boring as possible. For example, if you're at a party with somebody who triggers you, don't make any effort to connect with them. Instead, make yourself as boring as possible. Don't tell interesting stories that draw this person in, flatter them, or make yourself the center of attention. If they suggest you two should grab coffee sometime, just answer, "Yeah, we should." Then leave it at that. Narcissists thrive on the drama they can create and will move on to another victim when they can no longer get a rise out of you.[7]

Which ~~Edifying~~ Exploitative Spiritual Gathering is Right for You?

For those still looking to join a pious posse led by spiritual narcissists, here's a curated list of gatherings geared toward a wide range of starry-eyed believers:

A/theism in Action

Be a keyboard warrior in the rebirth and rebranding of the ongoing dialogue between believers (a.k.a. Christians) and heathens (a.k.a. atheists). Deconstruct with dudes. Create common ground with your fellow Pyrotheology pilgrims. Build bridges to nowhere. This seminal gathering will be held at a communal place that can hold space for philosophical pontificators in a spirit of mutuality and radical inclusion. (Note: this event has been canceled due to the inability to find any unspiritual sponsors.)

The Christian Copulation Conference

Celebrate National Masturbation Day (May 28th) by wanking as you worship. Explore Christian-Friendly Sex Positions (CFSP), participate in Jerk-offs for Jesus, do the Bible BDSM style, get a little left behind with a replay of Tim and Beverly LaHaye's sex videos, cut loose like Lentz, invite a spiritual wife to come at a theological threesome, swing it with Samson by doing it Delilah 'n' donkey style, learn how to be a beard for your beloved, and engage in shameless sex with parishioners. This evangelical eroticism will conclude with a swinging Song of Songs singalong. (Note: the "See How Your Megachurch Minister Measures Up" contest has been canceled due to too many #churchtoo cases.)

Cozy Creation Care Circles

Through an ongoing series of gatherings, spiritually minded armchair activists can stock up on the materials they need (all printed on recycled paper) so they can tackle climate change from the comfort of their couches. Savor sustainably sourced food, watered-down natural wine, and fair-trade coffee. (Sorry for the styrofoam. Supply chain issues.) Carbon offset credits will be available for purchase so that participants can remain creation-care conscious while also traveling in style. Similar cozy circles are being proposed for engaging in conversations around poverty, race, and affirming gays (and possibly lesbians).

The Cussing Christian Conference

Held on National Swear Day (January 31st), this conference offers keynote addresses from Muscular Christianity's branded biblical badasses, workshops with hipster pastors about how to market oneself as a tattooed theologian, cohorts to help remove the stains from spiritual and sexual sins committed in the quest for faith-based fame, a Swearology Smackdown whereby participants can practice their newfound soulful swearing skills, DIY ink stations, and a super-special display of preacher sneakers. The event concludes with a Stronger Men Demo replete with a biblical beard oil anointing ceremony, beyond the Bible branding, and pastoral piercings. (Due to the private nature of this event, media coverage will not be permitted. All conversations about slamming and swearing will take place via our private social media network.)

Flourish with the National Association of Evangelicals

Explore with fellow white evangelicals how to turn this biblical boat around by engaging in hard conversations on the toughest issues facing the church today. (Note: in light of the latest news surrounding a few too many of NEA's megachurch members, all sessions on #churchtoo have been canceled.)

Love from the Ashes

Be a part of a global transformational movement where human consciousness is being opened to its source of love and harmoniously integrate with other sentient kingdoms and dimensions. Drop inhibitions, banish boundaries, and cancel consent at this sex magick mystery school. Embrace the sacred whore within each one of us via tribal tantric-lite temple rituals in a celebration of questionable consensual-ish conscious sexuality.

Spiritual Lead(her) Unleashed

Is it time for you to wash your face, stop apologizing, and put your life together? If so, then purchase tickets to hear Christian motivational speakers, bloggers, and branded bestselling authors teach you how to promote boundless (yet toxic) positivity, commit plagiarism, and market your message via the MLM industry while controlling the conversation.

The Onward Christian Soldiers Pow-Wow

Get inspired by faith-filled patriots to "kill fear and, expose the truth," while appropriating Indigenous warrior language to justify your nativist beliefs. This revival features a rotating list of Christian crusaders chosen based on their rankings on Gettr, Gab, Parler, and Truth Social.

The Purity Conference
(sponsored by U-Turn Ministries)

Connect with non-fornicating fundamentalists for powerful teachings on patriarchy and purity culture, worship designed to get kids' pants on fire so they can receive a biblical anointing in their special place, and life-changing messages that empower young believers to live pure! Possible sponsors include the Council on Biblical Manhood and Womanhood, Joshua Generation Ministries, The Abstinence Clearing House, and Setting Captives Free: Purity Boot Camp.

The Way-Out Goosed Festival

Pick through this stale feast of passive-progressive Christian conversations designed to inspire with art, music, story, theater, spectacle, potluck protests, dude-led drumming circles, leftover liturgical dances, and recycled religion. With daisies. And didgeridoos. Plant-based pastoring. Cacao and Kumbaya. Conversations about kale. And Christianity. Fresh squeezed. Justice. Juice. Craft coffee. Homemade Kombucha. Homebrewers' meetup. Renaissance Faire clothing 4Sale. Branded beer 'n' hymns. Conservative-free zone.

#armchairactivist #Blacklivesmatter #BuyMyBook #Christianity21 #ChristianityLite #CraftChristian #CrappyChristian #DudesWith-Dreds #DrinkingDeconstruction #emergentchurchlives #faithafter-doubt #FaithfulAmerica #FaithForF*ckups #FlashingFoucault

#GayLesbianLivesMatter #GratefulGrounded #LGBTAlly #Home-brewedHomies #lovethesinnerandthesin #LoveWins #newkind-ofchristian #OnlineActivism #PyrotheologyPoser #rebootyourreli-gion #recoveringevangelcial #RecoveringWhiteSupremacist #RedStateRevival #RedLetterChristian #therevhunter #Spiritual-Wives #Spiritualwivesrock #theconfessionalpod #TheNewEvan-gelicals #TheNewMoralMajority #theologythatdoesntsuck #timandaprilshow #theologicaltriggers #theologybeercamp #VoteCommonGood[8]

4
Leaving Christianity?

I don't know exactly what I believe about God these days. But I know this: the Divine, if she exists, doesn't resemble my abuser. And if your spirituality feels like captivity, you're not losing faith, you're regaining freedom.

—Elise Heerde, *Holy Hell: Saved So Hard I Needed Therapy*[1]

In 2007 I was asked by the edgy imprint of what was then the world's largest Christian publisher to pen a book satirizing the New Atheists. I hesitated. After all, my beat focused on satirizing abuses within American Christianity (with an increasing emphasis on my own group, the progressive mainline church and Episcopalianism in particular). *Should I venture out of my lane by lampooning this newly branded anti-God movement?* I wondered.

My initial hunch was to say no, but then I thought back to a recent experience I had at the now defunct Book Expo 2006 where I caught Christopher Hitchens bellowing in all his drunken splendor. (I'm being kind here. This event was held at four p.m. on a Saturday when publishers were hosting happy hour, hoping to get folks sloshed enough to make sales, I suppose. Hitchens showed up more hammered than most.) Watching formerly faithful members of the flock praise one of the Four Horsemen of the Atheist Apocalypse for saving them from their fundy faith felt akin to watching the Christian circuses I had been covering for well over a decade. Maybe, just maybe, there might be something to satirizing these New Atheists. Besides, *The Wittenburg Door* was closing shop, and there were not enough other offerings on the table that would allow me to do things like pay rent and eat. So, I said yes to writing *The New Atheist Crusaders and Their Unholy Quest to Destroy Your Faith*.

But my reservations proved to be spot-on. Without going into details, I will tell you the publication of this book was a nightmare, in large part because the publisher who recruited me for the project somehow "forgot" to mention he would be leaving said edgy book imprint to form his own literary agency before the book's publication date. He also failed to disclose that my contract contained a morality clause whereby I'd have to return the advance should I engage in anything deemed "unbiblical." Not only was my book left out in the cold, but I was faced with the choice of agreeing to this morality clause or returning my advance. Given the ever-shrinking market for writing, I chose to publish over poverty, all the while being extra mindful not to engage in public acts of debauchery.

Once the book hit the market, the subsequent blowback I got from the atheist activist community told me I should have stayed in my lane. Suffice it to say that in my coverage of the evolution of secular spiritual communities, I was by no means the only one cyberbullied by some of those ex-evangelicals (named "exvangelicals" by Blake Chastain, host of the *Exvangelical* podcast). Yes, some ex-Christians get into the theological trenches and truly help other wounded warriors for Christ wage battle against their former beliefs. Others, such as those connected to "cutting-edge" Christian groups like the U.S. Emergent Church, become transformed into armchair atheists, deconstructionist dude bros, and other manly missionaries. Their unbiblical blather may sound more inclusive, but unpack their irreligious rubbish, and you'll find they're still mostly ribbing on Adam with just a token touch from Eve, while they take a few too many bites from the forbidden fruit. As reported by outlets such as *The Humanist,* the growing atheist/humanist movement has had its share of #metoo moments replete with the types of abuses uncovered by the growing #churchtoo movement.[2] These guys may have left the church, but they remain attached to the dynamics I've outlined in previous chapters that create scenarios ripe for spiritual narcissism to take over.

Yet ongoing media coverage focusing on the rise of "nones" coupled with the increase of humanist chaplaincies, atheist ministers, and books on how to live ethically outside the bounds of institutionalized religious systems told me there was also something positive to this trend of people seeking to live lives that are "good without God," to quote Greg Epstein, the first humanist chaplain at Harvard University.[3] So I continued my quest to seek out signs of secular spirituality, a journey I documented in my book *Roger Williams's Little Book of Virtues* for those interested in these explorations.

Often these humanist collectives resembled the emerging expressions of church I encountered in the U.K. and Europe that attracted those for whom church was not in their vocabulary but who wanted to connect via music, art, poetry, and other expressions that speak to their heart. Some ventures targeting ex-evangelicals, such as the U.K.-based Sunday Assembly, did not appeal to my tastes. I tend to prefer communal rituals over more hierarchical, preacher-centric events, especially when they are accompanied by happy-happy-joy-joy music. However, for the most part, I found these gatherings offered healthy alternatives for those who wanted to have a spiritual life sans either the Jesus junk or the anti-God rhetoric promoted by those on the extremes of the Christian versus atheist spiritual smackdown.

In my ongoing exploration of faith at the fringes, I observed how people continued to exit the institutional spiritual organizations that no longer speak to their hearts' desires. Some find occasional comfort in a church, synagogue, temple, or mosque that truly welcomes all and aims to be a place of healing rather than a means to exploit others. But an increasing number of spiritual seekers keep gravitating toward settings where they can worship, reflect, or meditate outside of traditional religious structures.

The more I connect with spiritual atheists, agnostics, religious exiles banished from the institutional church, and other consciousness explorers, both living and dead, the more I realize that while we all think for ourselves, we often speak a similar language at our core that connects us in our shared humanity. Through communal spiritual movements we can ignite a spark. That spark can create embers to fuel a fire. But first we need to get our matches in order.

When I was on the late John Shuck's podcast *The Progressive Spirit* on KBOO Portland Community Radio back in 2016, we chatted about the rise of alternative spiritual communities, "secular churches," so to speak. They aren't really churches; the participants wouldn't describe them as churches or as Christian, but they fill a void for those who left and even for some who never participated in church in the first place. These might be communities based on sacred dance, sexuality, improv, sustainable farming, or even cannabis and psychedelics. They may be connected to a particular church or faith community, but they're clearly not part of any larger institutional system. More than a club or an interest group, there is an ethic about them, a need to give something to the world, to touch the heart, to discover authenticity, to accept those left out, to care when someone in their community dies. To touch.[4]

These are groups that choose people over politics with the goal of creating communities where one can make unpretentious and accepting connections. While no group is perfect, the leaders strive to create a culture that respects others' boundaries and consent while holding each other accountable for their actions. Simply put, no one must buy into a pre-scripted partisan agenda or purchase specific products in order to join up.

With the Public Religion Research Institute (PRRI) reporting that "unaffiliated" is the only major religious category experiencing growth, you can expect to see an increase among those leaving institutional churches. The question remains: where will they go, and what kind of biblical baggage will they carry with them on their journey forward?[5]

Spirituality—at any level of integrity—speaks to deep human needs for meaning, purpose, and community. When people gather in these orbits, they bond through emotive rituals that create flow states and give access to neuroplastic changes in habits, beliefs, and priorities. The process can be beautiful and beneficial. But it can also amplify vulnerabilities and exploit good intentions.

—Derek Beres, Matthew Remski, and Julian Walker, *Conspirituality: How New Age Conspiracy Theories Became a Health Threat*[6]

5

Enlightened Energies or Predatory Posing?

Content warning: This chapter contains discussions about sacred sexuality that will very likely be disturbing (and possibly sinful) to those who consider themselves to have a biblical understanding of human sexuality. You might want to skip this chapter.

For survivors with unprocessed trauma around sexual abuse, be kind to yourself. If need be, come back and read this chapter when your body tells you you're ready.

Over the decades I've found both benefit and B.S. in explorations that connect body, mind, and soul in both Christian and non-Christian settings. I'm not looking to critique alternative religions and rituals per se, choosing to leave that work to therapists and scholars working in this field. Instead, I am

© Mayatoons[1]

simply noting instances where I see communities led by those promoting themselves as women-empowerment warriors, master mediators, and sacred sexual healers who display traits commonly found among spiritual narcissists.

In my decades of reporting on the weird, wild world of American Christianity, I've observed how often ex-Christians can easily transfer their worship of their pastor to a more secular spiritual shaman. This dynamic is particularly prevalent among those exiting high-control settings where they were taught by their leader to give their all to those in authority. Add to this their former church's often distorted teachings on the role of women in society and the human body, coupled with the absence of conversation around boundaries and consent in even the most liberated of church spaces, and no wonder many of those exiting authoritarian religious groups lack the tools needed to discern if a guru is godly or gross.

In *The Guru Papers: Masks of Authoritarian Power*, Joel Kramer and Diana Alstad ponder, "Are gurus, as they claim to be, a necessary doorway to religious experiences that make life more profound? Or rather, are they filling deep needs and thus inadvertently pointing to trouble spots and lacks in the fabric of our culture, as well as revealing the depth of our conditioning to want authorities and mistrust ourselves?"[2] The answer appears to be that it depends on the guru. For every Teresa of Avila, Thich Nhat Hanh, or Desmond Tutu whose work inspires humanity to seek out our better angels, there are also countless counterfeits proven to be hellish, not holy.

OK, I can hear the snickering off to the side about the wonkiness of taking the world of woo-woo too seriously. Yes, one can have a blast watching the latest social media goddess spouting gibberish as they demonstrate for their followers how to substitute crystals for Christianity. They might throw in a bit of pagan-esque prayers, a bit of Jungian junk, some Wiccan woo-woo, a bit of Teal tribe talk, a pseduoscientific review of the Marisa Peer Method,[3] and an unspiritual sprinkling of Gwyneth Paltrow's Goop-goo. Watch as they manifest the magick by transforming Reiki into a religion. But there's nothing funny about the dastardly dynamics present in some secular spiritual settings such as Agma Yoga, Bikram Yoga, the International School of Temple Arts (ISTA), Kundalini Yoga, neo-tantra pujas, NXIVM, OneTaste, and Shambhala Buddhism. Abuse is still no laughing matter within circles promising enlightenment while functioning more as pimps than prophets.[4]

Documentaries like *Wild Wild Country, The Vow,* and *Orgasm Inc.* may give one the illusion that predatory pushers hawking enlightenment like it's holy heroin represent a contemporary problem. But charismatic leaders promising their unique brand of salvation have sprung up throughout history, often during any time of social crisis and turmoil. A quick review of the U.S. points to metaphysical meanderings found in the nineteenth-century New Thought movement followed by the Positive Thinking movement led by Norman Vincent Peale (a.k.a. President Donald Trump's pastor) circa the 1950s, which then bled into the Age of Aquarius in the '60s.[5]

We're only beginning to explore the excesses that accompanied these periods of "enlightenment." I see scant documentaries profiling "casualties of the 60s," a term I coined to describe kids like me whose parents espoused free love, global peace, and universal condemnation of "The Man," all the while failing to provide a loving and stable home for their own children. My hippie parents embraced the Age of Aquarius with such abandon (until they died from alcohol- and drug-related conditions) that they kept forgetting they birthed three children in desperate need of actual parenting.

Only recently have I been able to look past its excesses and embrace fully the positive attributes of this free-for-all, peace-loving movement. To the best of my knowledge, my mother did not join my father when he participated in psychedelic explorations with Timothy Leary. Although I cannot verify the extent to which he joined in Leary's free-love frolics, given the voracity of his sexual appetite involving all genders, I strongly suspect he played along on some level—though he was also likely too passed out to participate. In hindsight, I should be grateful that my skepticism about my dad's quest for enlightenment, which was fueled more by Southern Comfort than spiritual gurus, safeguarded me from buying into the '80s New Age boom followed by the Oprah-esque endorsements of books like *The Secret* that led us to our current era of selling spiritual shlock via social media.

Top Ten Signs Your Godly Guru Is Actually a Spiritual SOB[6]

10. Holds sacred circles inside their echo chamber
9. Thinks boundaries are for babies
8. Manifests sex magick while on mushrooms 'n' MDMA*
7. They're predatorily perfect
6. Takes followers for a singularity ride along the spiritual bypass
5. Transforms their TM skills into Total Money
4. Trademarks their tantric touch
3. Favorite yoga position is the reacharound
2. Horny, not holistic
1. They're blind in their third eye

*For those not into party drugs, MDMA (3,4-Methylenedioxy-methamphetamine) is commonly known as ecstasy (tablet form) and molly (crystal form).

West Beats East

To understand the appeal of gurus for Westerners seeking to explore their sexuality from a spiritual lens, Kramer and Alstad note how we need to first understand the appeal of Eastern thought itself:

In addition to promises of experiencing cosmic consciousness, Eastern religions offer three elements that are particularly appealing to Westerners: 1) a perspective detached
from the involvements of individuated life that ultimately
sees everything as perfect; 2) practices that bring detach-
ment from emotions and worldly desires; and 3) in karma/
rebirth, a system that guarantees moral justice, the potential
of continual improvement, and an open-ended existence.[7]

These teachings attract spiritual adventurers who are all too willing to
push beyond their boundaries to prove their newfound liberation
from conventional norms. The more energy (and money) the disciple
invests in a given guru's offerings, the more likely they are to stick it
out no matter how godawful the guru may become or how confused
the disciple may feel. Any conflicts disciples have about submitting to
the guru's authority are defined pejoratively by the guru as resistance
to a higher truth, the intrusion of ego, or a sign of unwillingness to
give up attachments. The guru's pliant peeps chirp in agreement.

Since surrender initially alleviates conflict and can bring one a
sense of a pure state of divine bliss, giving up one's all to a higher
authority can become a powerful form of conditioning. Understandably, a follower in this state often attributes their positive feelings to
the guru's teachings while confusing any feelings of unconditional
love with the unconditional power the guru has over their disciples.
An authentic spiritual guide should recognize this pattern as transfer-
ence, a term used in psychotherapy to describe when a client redirects
their feelings about someone else onto their guide. Also, a legitimate
guide would recognize any feelings they may experience toward
someone under their care as countertransference and would have an
accountability system in place to help them process these emotions
appropriately.

Those gurus who either do not understand or choose to knowingly disregard this dynamic can easily misinterpret such positive emotions as being "karmically drawn" to a particular student. In this spirit they may even encourage their student to engage in sex with them as part of their process of achieving divine enlightenment. In Kramer and Alstad's estimation,

> At the heart of the ultimate trap is building and becoming attached to an image of oneself as having arrived at a state where self-delusion is no longer possible. This is the most treacherous form of self-delusion and a veritable breeding ground of hypocrisy and deception. It creates a feedback-proof system where the guru always needs to be right and cannot be open to being shown wrong—which is where learning comes from.[8]

Once the guru is viewed as hyper holy and thus immune to the corruption of power, Kramer and Alstad point to the types of abuse that can happen in scenarios involving individuals whose behaviors rise to the level of extreme narcissism. They include sexual abuse, material abuse, abuse of power, and self-abuse.

Now add into this equation the reality that too often a guru who exhibits these traits will isolate their followers, especially those deemed worthy enough to enter their supposedly sacred inner circle. So, even if a follower can recognize they are in a space that's more sadistic than spiritual, they often stay lest they lose their entire social network.

Sacred Sexuality Community or Super Scary Cult?

My experiences covering ISTA for *OnlySky* back in 2022 point to the difficulties in bringing abuses within sacred secular communities to light, especially those that focus on human sexuality. At first glance, their website appears to be full of New Age jargon that comes off more goofy than goddess-like and seems to be relatively harmless:

> ISTA is part of a global transformational movement where human consciousness is being opened to its source as love and harmoniously integrating with other sentient king-doms and dimensions. This movement functions not as an organization but as an organism led by a faculty consisting of facilitators, assistants, and apprentices.[9]

Even though there's a hierarchical structure within ISTA[10] along with the establishment of a 501(c)(3)[11] listing certain individuals as "being in charge," this organism claims to be leaderless. This lack of account-ability led to alleged abuses committed by members of ISTA's inner circle, including sexual assault and rape, especially by Baba Dez Nichols, founder of ISTA; Bruce Lyon, founder of Highden Temple; and Ohad Pele, founder of Kabala Love.

After my exposé on ISTA was published on the online humanist platform *OnlySky* on November 1, 2022, I received numerous mes-sages from others who participated in ISTA and were asking similar questions.[12] They encouraged me to investigate more alleged abuses within the ISTA network, such as ISTA's promotion of an event on their website titled "Wild Love: Love from the Ashes" hosted by Pele, with Lyon serving as a lead faculty member. This shamanic sh*t show was scheduled to take place July 13–19, 2020, at Auschwitz, the for-mer site of Nazi concentration and extermination camps in occupied Poland. However, the event was cancelled due to what was termed the "global pause" suddenly at play—a.k.a. the COVID-19 pandemic.

I mean seriously, WTF? Who in goddess's name thought it was a good idea to organize a sex festival against the backdrop of a former concentration camp? Yes, I've penned some theologically twisted material over the years. As my favorite countercultural icons Bill Hicks, Lenny Bruce, Richard Pryor, Mel Brooks, and Richard O'Brien (*The Rocky Horror Picture Show*) proved, even hot-button topics like religion, racism, antisemitism, and incest can be hysterical when handled by a comedic genius. But this was no dark comedy fictional flick—this was a real-life desecration of the dignity of those millions who entered this house of horrors during World War II.

Once my *OnlySky* editor said yes to an article exploring why ISTA would promote an event that read like a dismal attempt at a dark comedy sketch, I sent emails to those who were listed on the Wild Love webpage. In response, ISTA decided to sic their crisis PR representative in Israel on me. According to this rep, this "sexual shamanic journey" was not about *sex* but *love*:

> The retreat was not about "having sex at the death camps," as the letter tries to suggest, but about coming to the death camps with LOVE, respect and honor. They were planning to have vigils of silent meditation there in order to learn about the atrocities that happened there and feeling them deeply. They would do much of the work at the hostel out of the camp to move those heavy emotions using shamanic practices, heart sharings and rituals. The intention was to observe shadows, going deeply into the human conditioning of perpetrators versus victims. The intention was to work with the dehumanization of the other, that is happening in the perpetrators' minds, allowing them to act cruelly.[13]

Given this was not my first rodeo, I was accustomed to spiritual PR spin, but this response took devotional depravity to a whole new level. I'm all for self-expression—you do you—but there's a time and place for everything. An online search will reveal there's plenty of private homes rebranded as temples, sex clubs, and hedonistic themed retreats where consenting adults can engage in whatever alternative sexual practices turn them on. But using such a sacred site like Auschwitz as the inspiration for performing shamanic practices, heart sharing, and rituals (a.k.a. orgies) sounds more like a shock jock stunt than a genuine healing experience. On a practical level, an inquiry to the press office of the Auschwitz-Birkenau Memorial confirmed that this group lacked the necessary criteria needed to host any event at this site anyway.

After my piece, "Questioning a Shamanic Sex Camp in Auschwitz," was posted at *OnlySky* on January 23, 2023, the subsequent blowback I received from those loyal to ISTA was on par with the intense gaslighting I received while reporting on Christian charlatans for *The Wittenburg Door*.[14] Fortunately, as I had recently undergone EMDR, I was able to depersonalize their slams, and unlike during prior encounters with such narcissistic energies, I no longer felt triggered. Hence, I could respond clearly and objectively as I began to gather more stories from survivors of ISTA-related abuses.

Some former ISTA participants shared accounts of feeling coerced by the leaders in ways that point to a culture focusing on power, submission, and compliance. They reported feeling too over-stimulated and so food- and sleep-deprived that they did not feel they could opt out of the program without enduring considerable shame and ostracism from the group. The worst rituals referenced repeatedly by participants (emphasis on the plural) included sticking a carrot up one's rectum, engaging in nonconsensual sex with a male leader's "magic wand of light" as a means of achieving complete surrender, and sacrificing a live animal to then eat the flesh of their heart. It hardly needs to be said that these are textbook markers of a cult. If a spiritual sage can convince their devotees to do something their followers find to be repulsive, they now have loyal, obedient, and compliant disciples willing to do just about anything to please the group.

Pro tip: Unless one is part of an Indigenous tradition with a sacred connection to the earth and the cycles of nature, the mere suggestion of mostly white folks engaging in animal sacrifice speaks to an energy that's moved from dark to demonic. And if you're going to appropriate an Indigenous culture, have the common decency to list your actual sources instead of simply saying your rituals are performed with "respect and intention."[15] And for goddess' sake, if your organization's events require more than a few responses to concerns raised by participants, methinks your teaching strategy leaves much to be desired.[16]

Not surprisingly, I continued to get denigrated by those so addicted to their ISTA experiences that they could not see the myriad harms committed by select leaders who market their wares via the ISTA logo. This includes ancillary groups led by those with ISTA affiliations such as Awaken as Love, Empowered Pleasure, Highden Temple, Kabalove, The Pacific Northwest Tantra Festival Community! Facebook group, The Red Serpent Tantra School, Transform Into Love, the Tantra Not Trauma Facebook group, and the list goes on and on ad nauseam.[17]

In response to the rise of allegations made against select ISTA facilitators, ISTA did post an announcement on its website indicating several proposed changes.[18] Along these lines, a small volunteer group of survivors, allies, and activists from within the sacred sexuality, sex-positive, and neo-tantra communities came together to form Safer Sex-Positive & Spiritual Communities (3SC). As per their mission statement, the prime directive of their work is to make sex-positive and spiritual communities safer for all.[19] According to anecdotal accounts, some former ISTA participants have found genuine healing through the process of participating in 3SC, and changes appear to be underway, at least in some circles.

Still, stories of abuse keep spreading, like a virus that continues to infect the ISTA organism. While Nichols and ISTA parted ways in

2025, ISTA's "conscious completion" statement announcing this news focuses on honoring Nichols for his "contributions" while giving short shrift to the myriad concerns raised by multiple survivors.[20]

Despite their ongoing verbal responses to multiple concerns, news stories that paint ISTA in an unfavorable light fail to generate any substantial change.[21] For example, on the "Community" page listing the global leaders and organizers within ISTA, the pages for Lyon and Pele are no longer visible. But while they might be discretely removed from the "Community," their individual pages are still live and hosted on the ISTA website. Such misuse of sex magick coupled with their ongoing PR spin makes me wonder if the overall ethos of ISTA is more about protecting spiritual charlatans, if not outright predators, in their pursuit of power and pleasure than addressing the needs and concerns of the participants.

However, I am starting to see some sparks of hope that survivors of abuses in egregious settings that promised enlightenment and empowerment may find some semblance of justice. In 2025 Nicole Daedone and Rachel Cherwitz, founder and former head of sales for OneTaste Inc., respectively, were convicted of forced labor and human trafficking. Through the vehicle of OneTaste, Daedone promoted herself as a feminist icon, preaching the power of the female orgasm. But as former employees testified, these enlightened pioneers may have been promoting "female empowerment" but they were actually exploiting their female employees.

Also, NXIVM founder Keith Raniere was convicted in 2019 on seven counts, including racketeering, sex trafficking, forced labor conspiracy, and wire fraud conspiracy. While Raniere's public work focused on women seeking success through coaching and networking opportunities and was not sexual in nature, women in his programs were blackmailed, literally branded, near-starved, and enslaved—all in service to Raniere.

Coincidentally, the U.S. Attorney's Office for the Eastern District of New York tried both these cases. These verdicts point to signs that U.S. courts might be shifting their focus from blaming adult women for "allowing" themselves to become victimized in their quest for female empowerment and enlightenment toward holding abusers responsible for creating a coercive and controlling environment.[22]

Sexual Healing or Shamanic Harm?

A trained guide can be a valuable companion in helping seekers open up their sexuality by connecting body, mind, and spirit. As I noted in an article for *Spirituality & Health* titled "How Tantra Connects Sexuality and Spirituality," while anyone can make these connections by themselves, sometimes the activation of sexual energy and the opening of the heart, pineal gland, and other subtle body phenomena is often easier and more explicit when exploring one's sexual side with a trusted, compatible person.[23] As Gwenn Cody, a sex-positive therapist, observes, humans often have complicated and conflicted feelings about idealizing others: "It's built into our primate heritage to long for leaders to follow." However, Cody delineates between authentic visionaries and narcissistic leaders as follows:[24]

Authentic visionary leaders have these hallmarks:

- ❑ Confidence
- ❑ Thinking outside the box/risk-taking
- ❑ Vision
- ❑ Determination
- ❑ Powerful communication skills

Conversely, narcissistic leaders possess these behaviors:

- ❑ Grandiosity
- ❑ Entitlement
- ❑ Manipulative communication skills

❏   Aggressively determined to prevail

❏   Excessively self-confident and risk-seeking[25]

As these traits can look remarkably similar at first glance when you are looking to explore your sexuality, here's some necessary homework you should do to ensure you are entrusting yourself to a qualified guide versus a predatory guru.[26] This same homework can also be applied by those trying to discern if a particular guru's claims come off as healing or full of hot air:

❏   Google the guide (start with "[Name of guide] and abuse" and see if anything pops up). In addition, find social media groups, like Facebook groups, where spiritual guides advertise their services and participants share their experiences with specific gurus. But caveat emptor—let the buyer beware; employ the same care you would when seeking out any qualified health care professional. Also, bear in mind that not all discussion groups are created equal, and some of them harbor individuals known to be problematic (and worse) within the sex-positive community. But you can still ask the people in these groups in general whether a spiritual guide is safe. Having someone say that a spiritual guide is safe doesn't guarantee that they're safe. On the other hand, if there are any negative reports about someone, then that's a warning sign to be taken seriously.

❏   Peruse the guide's books, websites, social media feeds, podcasts, and other forms of media. Does their work build upon the existing work within their tradition, including citing their sources and using psychological terminology correctly? Or do they make bare assertions and false claims while quoting meaningless, made-up jargon that they fail to adequately define? Step back should you spot them dancing the Malignant Mash by mangling Eastern teachings, making up pseudo-psychological terms, and spouting meaningless spiritual sayings until they conjure up an inedible word salad. And in the spirit of Monty Python, "Run away!" should the guide claim to have a charisma that allows them to speak on behalf of the divine or receive transmissions from some mythical being.

☐ Check any credentials they tack on at the end of their name. This includes researching any schools or individual teachers they cite so you can verify the legitimacy of their training as well as ascertaining whether they studied under spiritual leaders whose practices are more terrifying than tantric. This research can be a tad tricky since those claiming to be sexual healers often give themselves enlightened names like Amara, Baba, Crystal, Devi, Love, and Joy. Unfortunately, many also flaunt made-up credentials that they sprinkle around like magical fairy dust designed to give the illusion they are qualified experts. Those spiritual souls with a genuine interest in this work will present themselves honestly and with integrity. They don't need to mislead others, unlike a spiritual narcissist.

☐ Licensing doesn't necessarily mean enlightening. I've noted my experiences elsewhere in this book with licensed clinical therapists who abused their positions of influence and authority. In contrast, many people working as sacred sexual healers are unlicensed, as their work falls beyond what clinical licensing boards (and insurance companies) will sanction. Licensed or not, any qualified guide will offer an explanation of any training they've had, with references to boot. What do former students, their teachers, and colleagues say about this guide? Watch their body language for signs of discomfort while answering inquiries, especially if their comments are made in a group setting where there may be pressure to present with a positive persona.

❑ How does this particular guide talk about others working in the sacred sexuality field? Do they at least acknowledge the value others outside of their inner circle bring to this work, or do they demean them as being inferior and incompetent?

❑ Is the guide or their assistant available to answer any questions before you sign up for their offerings? If it's impossible to chat with anyone before forking over your funds, assume you are dealing with someone too "busy" to be bothered. Move on. Next.

❑ Audit a class or workshop. Watch how they interact with students and check whether the event description is in sync with what is transpiring at the event. Does your experience match up with their marketing? If auditing is not possible, be sure to create an exit plan where you can safely leave if necessary.

❑ Do they hide their mistreatment of others behind claims of female empowerment, respect for Indigenous cultures, embracing alternative lifestyles, and solidarity with 2SLGBTQIA+[27] folx, only to then call those questioning their abusive practices prudes (and worse)?

❑ When a participant raises a concern, are they treated with care and compassion? Or do they get dismissed with vague platitudes like "If you were more enlightened, you'd understand what we're doing here," "That's just your interpretation," "Don't let yourselves fall into the trap of victimhood," "There's no good or bad in this world of non-duality," or "We're all about universal love, so just surrender to the experience"?

❑ Are survivors and their allies believed when they report instances of physical or sexual abuse, or are they ostracized from the group—or worse, accused of launching a witch hunt? Be very wary if the leaders spout off about "sovereignty" by claiming participants are solely responsible for everything that happens to them while they are under the leaders' care, adding, "There are no victims." A legitimate professional working in the sacred sexuality field will have a system set up to hold themselves accountable for their behavior. Also, I can count on one hand the number of false reports of sexual assault in spiritual settings I've heard over the past thirty-some-odd years. On the other hand, I've lost track of the number of those who spoke about their abuse but never got justice.

❑ How do this guide and their followers respond when you say no to any component of their program? Do you feel your boundaries are respected, or are you pressured to go with the flow on the grounds that by sitting out a particular activity, you're "letting the group down?" This is a particular concern when doing "encounter group" sorts of activities that involve aggression, violence, or disclosing highly personal information in public. A non-narcissist guide may gently prod participants to go outside of their comfort zones and explore their "edges." However, they will also support your boundaries and will not force you into nonconsensual activities, especially those that present ethical and even legal obstacles. They certainly won't deprive participants of the basics such as sleep, food, clothes, and water, along with critical documents such as passports, driver's licenses, and a means to leave.

❑ Be mindful of how power dynamics can muddy consent. Approach with extreme caution any scenarios where leaders participate in their events or appear to use them as opportunities to secure potential partners. If they propose that the only way through enlightenment is through sexual contact with them, just know you're likely dealing with a serial predator. If a truly enlightened guide finds themselves attracted to a student, they will process these feelings appropriately and seek professional help as warranted. If they wish to pursue a connection with a particular individual, they will remove themselves from serving as this person's teacher and then allow enough time for the power dynamics to dissipate.

❑ Follow the money. Yes, qualified coaches should be paid for their time and talents, but be mindful lest their primary motivation appears to be pleasure and profit for themselves and their inner circle. Notice if the focus shifts from celebrating the community to following a select group of leaders. This often happens when the group morphs from a meetup or a grassroots collective of like-minded souls into an LLC or 501(c)(3) nonprofit.

❑ Are those who volunteer their time treated with care and respect as valued members of the community—or viewed as the "help" (a.k.a. free labor)?

❑ Yes, psychedelics can be mind-blowing (to put it mildly) when done in a safe and trusted setting—but find the nearest exit if the event hosts show up visibly altered or if you hear rumors from trustworthy sources that they are plying potential partners with party drugs. Just go. As. In. Now.

❑ Run if you spot signs of trophy hunting, such as keeping detailed lists of their sexual conquests or bragging about their past conquests like they're auditioning for the latest episode of *Gurus Gone Wild!* Yes, yes, yes, I know their vibe sounds so playful, they make you purr. You've never been this blissed out. And the crowd is just so enraptured. But trust me, they're more Stepford Wives than spiritual goddesses. Before you get lobotomized, leave. Yes, the trauma-bonded babes will go all metaphysical mean girl on you for busting their blissed-out bubble. If you can't get rid of that nagging feeling you must go back, please connect with a trauma-informed therapist who can help you break your bonds to this

B.S. Note: I've used gender-neutral pronouns in describing predatory gurus as stories abound of spiritual leaders of all genders displaying signs of extreme narcissism. But this on-the-prowl quest for mostly women but occasionally men represents a peculiar dynamic I've seen almost exclusively among those men who seem to take the whole Robert Bly inner warrior myth a bit too far.

❏ Do they require a non-disclosure agreement (NDA) before you can play? Nope, nada, no way. An NDA tends to be described by event hosts as a way to keep the community safe. In reality, it's a tool used to suppress any claims of abuse. A qualified guide will discuss the importance of confidentiality, similar to how AA meetings stress "what is said here stays here" for the sake of protecting the privacy of those baring their souls, but they will never ask you to refrain from speaking out should you notice signs that something is amiss.

❏ Be wary of any organization that downplays how narcissism plays out in sacred sexuality settings.[28] That should tell you they're more into woo-woo than wellness.

❏ Finally, for those looking for additional information on exploring sacred sexuality in a healthy holistic setting, intimacy coach Wilrieke Sophia has recommendations on both their website[29] and their useful "Red Flags in Workshops" document.[30]

Classical Tantra vs. Neo-Tantra, a.k.a. Let the Battle of the Sexes Begin (or Maybe Not)

When I first began exploring how to integrate my spirituality and my sexuality, the word "tantra" kept popping up. Over the years, I learned that those I met who talked the tantra talk were referring to neo-tantra and not classical tantra traditions. I can see in hindsight how distinguishing between classical and modern tantra would have benefited me greatly in my spiritual walk.

In a nutshell, when exploring tantric practices, be mindful that "tantra" originally referred to a text or treaty, though many Western practitioners translate "tantra" as "weave" or "warp." Elements of classical tantra are pre-Vedic (fourth millennium BCE), with tantric texts emerging in the sixth century BCE with a focus on spirituality not sexuality.

In comparison, neo-tantric practices that focus almost exclusively on sexual acts, such as tantric massage, can be traced to San Francisco and "Oom the Omnipotent" (Pierre Bernard) in the early 1900s. This work was then refined, starting in the 1960s, in neo-tantra books that mix different traditions such as Hinduism (chakras, kundalini energy), Taoism (ting and yang), and Mahayana Buddhist tradition (compassion).

For those looking to enhance their sex life via neo-tantric techniques, vet potential teachers with care, and enjoy the journey. Just don't kid yourself that what you're being taught is connected to an ancient Indian practice despite the presence of temple trappings, Kali conversations, and other signs of cultural appropriation.

Despite a few too many gurus in the neo-tantric circuit claiming they possess the divine portal required to achieve complete enlightenment, tantra is really timeless. Going deep into it beyond just that neo-tantra gateway via sex can open up new dimensions for inner transformation using tantra meditation that connects body, mind, and spirit. When I'm in this state of interconnectedness, I find I can then reach out and connect with others and nature itself more fully and completely.[31]

When a Sexual Haven Becomes a Prison: A Culty Conversation with *Cult Trip* Author Anke Richter

---

We all want to belong to something greater than ourselves. To be accepted by like-minded people. We all want to believe that our ideas about the world are the ultimate truth of the universe. Cults are that straightforward: purpose, community, and understanding how the world works. Who doesn't want all these things?

—J. W. Ocker, *Cult Following: The Extreme Sects That Capture Our Imaginations—and Take Over Our Lives*[32]

When psychologists reference cult leaders, they often speak of the "dark triad." This phrase pertains to the personality traits of narcissism, psychopathy/sociopathy, and Machiavellianism.[33] As defined elsewhere, those spiritual leaders who display signs of the first two traits most likely would fall into the category of an extreme narcissist, but for them to rise to the status of cult leader, their behaviors need to escalate from malignancy to Machiavellianism.

For those who are too happy-happy-joy-joy to delve into the self-centered scribblings of Italian statesman and writer Niccolò di Bernardo dei Machiavelli (1469–1527) in his best-known work, *Il Principe* (*The Prince*), he presents a view of the world that might even make Ayn Rand run away. Machiavelli's view is that politics is amoral and that ordinarily unscrupulous actions involving deceit, treachery, and violence are permissible as effective means of acquiring and maintaining political power. Thus, Machiavellianism signifies egregiously immoral behavior that serves one person or group's self-interest rather than the greater good of a community or country.[34]

Even though interacting with extreme narcissistic energies can be quite draining, very few spiritual leaders fitting the clinical definition for clinical narcissism will actually morph into a missional Machiavellian. Even if they're risen to the level of religious rock star, somehow they lack the stomach to sign a deal with the devil. A true missional Machiavellian will amass enough godly groupies (e.g., ultimate enablers) that allow them to live lawlessly like Lucifer. For those wondering if the spiritual narcissist(s) in their life might have risen to the level of cult-like status, I recommend doing actual research beyond simply scrolling social media and streaming services. Much of what's out there constitutes "cult porn" designed to titillate, not educate.

To help me point folks in the right direction and to better determine if a given run-of-the-mill malignant narcissistic leader also qualifies as a cult god, I decided to connect with journalist Anke Richter, author of *Cult Trip: Inside the World of Coercion and Control*, about her investigation into sex cults.[35] (Yes, not every cult focuses on S-E-X, but the concept of giving up one's bodily autonomy in service to a group is a dynamic found in every cult.) Since penning her book, Richter has gone on to organize Decult 2024, a New Zealand-based conference focusing on abuses in church and spiritual settings. This conference's twenty sessions ranged from Jehovah's Witnesses to ISTA plus the first MISA survivor speaking out publicly.[36] Richter is also planning a podcast, a documentary, and future Decult conferences. Our conversations flowed so organically that it feels natural for me to simply note these reflections as they happened in what follows.

How do you define a cult?

A less controversial word for "cult" is "high-control group." According to experts like Dr. Janja Lalich, these groups have an all-encompassing belief system. So in a tantric yoga cult like Agama, you have specific and outlandish views, for instance, about medicine or sexual healing, that cannot be questioned. Or in Scientology, there are teachings against psychiatry, hence the groupthink and a lack of internal criticism. But it's not their beliefs that are so problematic, but the systems of power and control. There's usually a promise of life-changing personal transformation by a charismatic and often narcissistic leader. They see the outside world as evil or less evolved—us versus them. Love bombing, gaslighting, spiritual bypassing, secrecy about the program, a lot of volunteer work, or high fees to climb the ranks and stay involved are also typical markers. What initially feels like a haven eventually becomes a prison.

Why is "cult" considered to be such a debatable term?

This term is only debatable by cult apologists who like to speak of "new religious movements" instead. I'm also amazed that people who've never been harmed in cults or researched them think it's up to their own and often incorrect definition—imagine how that would work for framing sexual assault, for instance. It would be unacceptable. After *Cult Trip* came out, I heard from a former spin doctor for Harvey Weinstein who did crisis PR for OneTaste. He thinks an organization is only a cult if you can't physically leave, which I've also been told by an alleged sexual abuser and lead teacher in ISTA. There are so many misconceptions out there—like the assumption that people in cults are weak, lost, uneducated, or stupid.

Why is the assumption that those who join cults are losers simply not true?

We're all susceptible to getting hooked if something speaks to us at the right time. Cults usually have some good content in the mix, and they attract people with open hearts and minds: idealistic seekers for a better world who get exploited further down the track and often turn into fanatics, recruiters, and spiritual abusers themselves. The most vulnerable time for someone to get hooked into a coercive group is after changing jobs or leaving home, and starting at college, or the death of a loved one. These are not human failures or weaknesses but very normal circumstances.

How did you choose the cults that you profiled in *Cult Trip*?

Centrepoint was a former "free love" and therapy cult from the Human Potential Movement in the 1980s in New Zealand where I live. This cult was unmatched even on a global scale.[37] They held drug sessions with families, and every third child there has been sexually abused. I stumbled onto its aftermath when I met a former teenager from Centrepoint at a conscious sexuality festival in Australia. Over the years, I became an accidental sex cult tourist myself and visited OneTaste in San Francisco, The New Tantra (TNT) in the Netherlands, Osho's former ashram in India, and Agama Yoga in Thailand.[38]

Were you participating in those cults too?

Not at Agama, but I had skin in the game because I was dabbling in shamanic courses at the time with ISTA. Despite my research, it took me a long time to see it for what it was. That realization was also part of my personal cult trip and is in the book: the journalist who came too close. I'm still figuring out what drew me in. Although I don't identify as a victim and wasn't harmed, I can relate to the conflicting feelings of grief, loss, and shame that cult leavers grapple with because of the spiritual manipulation.

Gloriavale, a fundamentalist Christian enclave where women are treated as breeding machines, became another investigation of yours.[39] What characteristics did this group and the more free-spirited Centrepoint have in common in terms of their approach to sexuality?

Too many women, and their children, suffered sexual abuse there—a mainstay of cults. Both New Zealand leaders—Hopeful Christian of

Gloriavale and Bert Potter of Centrepoint—were paedocriminals and went to jail.[40] I only made the connection at the end of my ten-year research that Gloriavale, a strictly monogamous Christian enclave that looks like Gilead from *The Handmaid's Tale,* is a sex cult as well. Sexuality plays a central role there, like it did at Centrepoint where the doctrine was promiscuity. These leaders define what their people's sex lives should look like, how it should be done, how often, and with whom. The pressure to be sexually available, whether for the whole group or your husband in an arranged marriage, can be just as abusive as the punishment and shaming of someone's libido. It especially messes with children in puberty.

What did you observe in your reporting that makes ex-Christians particularly susceptible to sacred sexuality cults?

It's the promise of liberation from shame, fear, and guilt around their desire and sexual identity. Healing the damage caused by purity culture. A lot of social media recruitment into neo-tantra now targets former evangelicals. But while it can be helpful to undo religious indoctrination in these cathartic trainings, participants might experience a new kind of undue influence there and become conformist and brainwashed again. Another attraction is the new sense of belonging: finding a community that offers the comfort of a church group—with a temple that celebrates sexual connection. The new tribe replaces the family of origin, which many shunned exvangelicals also lost when they left the religion.

Briefly describe what a "workshop high" is and how this dynamic can impact one's ability to fully consent to the activities being presented.

Large Group Awareness Trainings (LGATs) such as Landmark and ISTA have been studied and demystified by academics like the late Margaret Singer or more recently John Hunter.[41] In a weeklong 24/7 training full of rituals, circle confessions, and cathartic release, a cocktail of brain chemicals floods your system and clouds your thinking. Constantly "dropping the mind" while you're loved up or turned on can result in overriding your inner "yes" or "no," especially if past trauma is retriggered. It's like being on drugs—I've been there myself. And if you crave a desired outcome like the rest of the group and paid a lot of money for it, then you probably won't speak up when something doesn't feel right—especially if you don't want to be labeled as "acting from your wounding" or "stuck in victim consciousness."

Why do you say in your book, "In a hierarchical high-control group, open relationships are completely at odds with consensual non-monogamy"?

I've come across former Centrepoint members who endured years of pressure to sleep with as many group members as possible. Their boundaries were pushed and violated and their instincts overridden. There wasn't much freedom in their "free love" commune, but plenty of manipulation.[42] Sex became a commodity and a dogma. Consent can only be freely given between equals, not under pressure. Despite the sex gurus' constant preaching of "loving," their reign doesn't represent polyamory, but sexual coercion.

As a reporter, how do you deal with what you described as a moral dilemma—when does someone's truth that needs to be heard add to another person's trauma and pain?

I don't have the perfect answer for that, but I believe in what the Germans call "Vergangenheitsbewältigung" (coming to terms with the past). That can only happen by looking at the painful truth, not by shoving it under the carpet. It gets difficult, though, when a perpetrator has a family. Exposing his awful actions also means that his children suffer further from the stigma. My first attempt at writing a book about Centrepoint failed because it became too conflicting and impacted my mental health. I was dealing with so much unresolved trauma and with people who panicked or threatened me legally. Others desperately wanted their stories told. I stepped into a cesspool of unresolved trauma.

How do you view those who are still perpetuating the abuses despite reporting from you and others?

We now know that child abuse was as rampant in the Osho communes, from Pune to Medina to Rajneeshpuram, as it was at Centrepoint, and that the guru was a rapist. Same ideology with the same disastrous consequences. But to my knowledge, none of over a hundred perpetrators have been brought to justice yet. That needs to happen, and Sarito Carroll's recent book, *In the Shadow of Enlightenment*, is an eye-opener which every Sannyasin should read.[43] (For those not tuned into Hindu culture, "Sannyasin" is a Sanskrit word that describes someone who has reached the life stage of "sannyasa", or "renouncement of material possession."[44]) At least the Romanian founder of MISA—the umbrella organization of tantra yoga schools like Tara in the U.K. and Natha in Scandinavia— has finally been arrested,[45] but the head of Agama Yoga hasn't. Too many sex gurus are still flying under the radar or are whitewashing their actions and silencing critical voices. Cults are litigious.

What about their followers who are enabling the abuse?

I'm not excusing their actions, but I feel for idealistic people who get sucked into a group where they're pushed to override their inner moral compass and do things they wouldn't have done otherwise. They're also cult victims even while they've harmed others. The first step for their rehabilitation and collective healing can be an apology to the survivors, listening to them, and getting involved in a process of reconciliation and accountability. The Centrepoint Restoration Project and their open letter is a good example of that.[46] Decult, which I started last year, is part of that conversation too.

Would you participate again in those settings?

Those days are definitely over. My innocence is long gone, and my B.S. radar is on high alert—I wouldn't be a happy student. I cringe at the cultural appropriation and gender stereotypes that are rife in this field. And while I appreciate that many people have benefited from neo-tantra or so-called sexual shamanism, I now believe less is more. Instead of flying around the world from one extreme training to another, handing over your money and eventually your freedom of mind to a suspect "school" with grandiose promises of evolutionary transformation, how about creating a more consent-based, sex-positive, holistic culture in your own community instead? I see that happening with some younger people in the alternative festival scene, and it gives me hope. If we can normalize sex education and freedom of expression, if we can bring desire and intimacy out of the shadow, then we take away the power of cults who monetize and exploit this important part of our humanity.

© *The Wittenburg Door*[47]

From the crafty redefinition of existing words (and the invention of new ones) to powerful euphemisms, secret codes, renamings, buzzwords, chants, and mantras, "speaking in tongues," forced silence, even hashtags, language is the key means by which all degrees of cultlike influence occur. Exploitative spiritual gurus know this, but so do pyramid schemers, politicians, CEOs of start-ups, online conspiracy theorists, workout instructors, and even social media influencers. In both positive ways and shadowy ones, "cult language" is, in fact, something we hear and are swayed by every single day. Our speech in regular life—at work, in Spin class, on Instagram—is evidence of our varying degrees of "cult" membership. You just have to know what to listen for.

—Amanda Montell, *Cultish: The Language of Fanaticism*[48]

6

Breaking the Cycle: Goodness, Not Gaslighting

It turned out that this man worked for the Dalai Lama. And he said—gently—that they believe when a lot of things start going wrong all at once, it is to protect something big and lovely that is trying to get itself born—and that this something needs for you to be distracted so that it can be born as perfectly as possible.

—Anne Lamott, *Traveling Mercies: Some Thoughts on Faith*[1]

In the previously mentioned *The New Science of Narcissism,* W. Keith Campbell shares research that appears to show people wising up and pushing back against narcissism. While popular narcissistic global leaders continue to rise in prominence, people are now calling out paid celebrity endorsements of candidates and shifting away from influencer-driven social media as they look to make more genuine connections. Campbell admits a move toward a world less focused on status and more focused on creativity is but pure speculation at this juncture, though he has hope:

> During this next decade, I envision the pendulum swinging back. The prolific 2000s-era narcissism will fade as more people recognize and reject the phoniness of our narcissistic leaders who rose to power and failed in their leadership.

Fame is more fleeting now than ever, and people are waking up to that fact.

We're turning back to self-care, renewal, and smaller communities built on personal connections. We're seeking happiness, and true happiness is ultimately built on love and genuine relationships. The fact that we're seeking the new, the different, and the authentic means we have the ability to shift away from harmful behaviors and lifestyles. Although this shift may take time, it's heading in the right direction.[2]

Concurrent with this trend, psychologist Lisa Miller observed in her book *The Awakened Brain* how each one of us is endowed with a natural capacity to perceive a greater reality and consciously connect to the life force that moves in, through, and around us. She reflects, "Whether or not we participate in a spiritual practice or adhere to a faith tradition, whether or not we identify as religious or spiritual, our brain has a natural inclination toward and docking station for spiritual awareness. The awakened brain is the neural circuitry that allows us to

see the world more fully and thus enhance our individual, societal, and global well-being."[3]

While this research is still in the nascent stages, Miller's work points to the potential for us to tap into our innate spirituality. That is, if we can get out of our heads and connect with others via our hearts.

© Becky Garrison

Seeker, Heal Thyself

While this emerging research into narcissism sounds quite promising, Rev. Kurt Neilson, retired chaplain and author of *Urban Iona*, reminds me that leadership and community character are only part of the equation. "An essential piece of searching for a healthy community is for the searcher to do their own work and be clear about what needs they bring to spiritual settings," he opines.[4]

In my ongoing conversations with futurist Brad Sargent, we continue to explore why spiritual pilgrims such as ourselves keep holding on to this elusive hope of one day finding a heavenly kingdom here on earth. We both began our spiritual journeys in the '70s and '80s when there were no books on spiritual abuse, religious trauma, or narcissism. Heck, the alcohol and addiction recovery movement was just getting going.

Fortunately, as Sargent is wired to do pattern recognition, he can make connections sans research data when examining his history of participating in toxic, dysfunctional church settings. He noticed that while each church setting he encountered might be different in terms of their theology, their tactics followed a similar playbook, with the leaders and those within their inner circles projecting themselves as the voice of Jesus.

People like Sargent who want to make an impact as righteous Christians by doing the right thing can be particular magnets for such leaders. "They promised what would happen. Such promises weren't made overtly but with more covert affirmations like, 'You're doing something important' and 'You're helping the cause,'" he remembers.

Sargent offers this reflection made by his college friend Linda O., whom he met when both of them endured the same horrific church split in the 1970s. "Manipulators and martyrs go together in matched pairs." This implosion led Sargent to begin his lifelong quest to research and expose church abuses. As much as we might want to blame those who manipulated us to go against our better judgment, Sargent suggests we look inside first: "There's a dark and a light wolf inside of each of us. The one you feed is the one that's going to win." This is not to justify or minimize spiritual abuses but to suggest that we engage in self-examination should we keep finding ourselves in spiritually abusive settings. Why put ourselves through such misery again and again and again?

Sargent suggests we ask, "What am I seeking that draws me to this group?"[5] When I answer this question for myself as a spiritual pilgrim, I can see a pattern whereby in my quest for a chosen family to replace my biological one, I ignored enough red flags to rival any Fourth of July blowout. This knowledge helps keep me sane instead of smacking my head whenever I reflect on the spiritual snafus I've created along the way. No more should-ing all over myself anymore. None of this doing the "would've, could've, should've" dance by wondering how things might be if only I had done A, B, and C instead of X, Y, and Z. *Stop dreaming and dancing; keep calm and stand your ground*, I tell myself.

Healing from Spiritual Narcissists

Courtesy of Jill Leigh, founder and director of The Energy Healing Institute

1. Do the work of understanding what attracted you to the individual(s) who love bombed you spiritually. There are a lot of reasons you were pulled into their orbit. Unless you dig in and find out what those bright shiny objects were that you found irresistible, you're at risk of being pulled in again! Here's what people commonly discover when they perform an inner inquiry. They're often seduced by the:

❑ Promise of unrealistic gains, such as attaining enlightenment, true abundance, ascension, or other spiritually lofty
ideals that are never easily achieved or bestowed by
another

❑ Magnetism of the personality, in spite of the underlying
twinges of worry, concern, or even downright mistrust of
the individual and/or their teachings

❑ Glow of the attention paid to them as an initiate, devo-
tee, mentee, or member of the group, practice, church, or
fellowship

❑ Need to feel whole, healed, evolved, spiritual, uplifted,
special, gifted—or any other adjective that creates a sense
of elevation and leveling up

2. Learn about sovereignty and autonomy. This is a far deeper
and more elevating topic than any of the hollow spiritual
promises that are easily made and often not kept. No one
can take away your sovereignty or autonomy. It's a universal
principle. The fact is, you're either sovereign . . . or you're not.
If you're not sovereign, you're potentially easily led—to wherever someone else might want to take you. Lacking sovereignty means that you are not in control of yourself; you are
not aware of being infiltrated with someone else's energy
and intentions. It can certainly enable others to victimize
you, to usurp your authority with their own agenda.

3. Remember that sovereignty creates ownership—of your life,
your experiences, and equally importantly, your energy.
Have you ever played the game where you stand with one
foot behind the other, heel to toe, with a partner doing the
same? Your lead foot touches your partner's foot, and with
your hands, you push on your partner's hands to see if you
can knock them off balance. Whoever is the most grounded,
has the most engaged core strength and the most solid balance, is going to win, every time. Energetic sovereignty is

like that. It's a state of grounded awareness, containment, and inner alignment. It creates individuation and distinction and holds you in your space.

4. When you do the inner work of uncovering what drew you into the spiritual narcissist's orbit and you make it your choice and your job to resolve the energetic imbalance within you, sovereignty becomes your guiding principle. It repels narcissists and provides you with clarity and alignment to consciously choose the people whom you'll entrust with your spiritual awareness. And it's a much simpler way to gain spiritual mastery![6]

In recent years I've become increasingly aware of the gift of time. For example, after exiting a sex-positive community that had become riddled with abuse, I felt a strong, understandable sense of abandonment. But rather than rush into finding another group to meet my need for family, I took the recommendation of a trusted therapist to wait at least a year after exiting a toxic community before finding a healthy one. This time helped ensure that I healed myself enough to avoid repeating the spiritual spin cycle (or at least it kept me from spinning around quite so fast that my critical thinking skills would end up by the side of the road).

No religion, no political ideology, no war nor revolution has ever been as conducive to progress as this simple notion: that we should treat our assumptions with skepticism and stay open to new ideas and information. It's a paradigm that has the massive advantage of baked-in fluidity and—across the long arc—incremental improvement. It facilitates memetic evolution. It is fundamentally anti-doctrinal, demanding of us epistemic, intellectual, psychological, neurological, and cultural humility. (Postmodernism, to its credit, contributed much to that last one.)

Stir in a couple of ideas like the Principle of Charity (listening to the views of others with the generosity you'd like to be listened to) and a dedication to rejecting in-group/out-group thinking, and you've got yourself a sweet little recipe for societal flourishing.

Old bathwater, evergreen babies, baby.

—Tim Minchin, *You Don't Have to Have a Dream: Advice for the Incrementally Ambitious*[7]

But Their Work Healed Me!

The late Tibetan Buddhist spiritual leader and founder of Shambhala Buddhism Chögyam Trungpa Rinpoche (1939–1987) wrote in his seminal tome *Cutting Through Spiritual Materialism*, "Walking the spiritual path properly is a very subtle process; it is not something to jump into naively. There are numerous sidetracks which lead to a distorted, ego-centered version of spirituality; we can deceive ourselves into thinking we are developing spirituality when instead we are strengthening our egocentricity through spiritual techniques."[8] Yet his son, Sakyong Mipham Rinpoche, failed to practice what his father preached. Following Sakyong's death in 2018, it became known that he had committed multiple abuses.[9] As I researched this chapter, Chögyam Trungpa's name came up frequently in the works of spiritual teachers, but in light of the revelations about his son, I chose not to include works penned by those who praised Chögyam Trungpa and have yet to retract their endorsement or acknowledge the abuses committed by Sakyong and others within his circle. Without such praise from highly regarded, enlightened spiritual teachers, Shambhala Buddhism would not have grown into the international movement it is. Not surprisingly, I had to omit a few other authors I had planned to quote after I learned of multiple survivors speaking up about abuses that remain unaddressed as of this writing.

This raises the question of what to do with the works penned by a leader whose teachings touched so many souls on levels ranging from profound to predatory. Right now, I don't have a solid answer. Where do we find reliable signs of genuine goodness? Removing their works only serves to create a revisionist history. We cannot learn from past mistakes if they've been completely erased from the books (though, trust me, the abuse remains very much in the minds of those impacted), but exalting the work of unreliable guides without acknowledging the harm they've done does not serve justice either.

In *You're Not the Problem: The Impact of Narcissism and Emotional Abuse and How to Heal*, Helen Villiers and Katie McKenna note how very often the narcissist will make it seem they are more hurt than you are: "They will make themselves the victim: 'I'm the worst person ever.' 'You should just leave me.' 'I can't do anything right!' 'I just won't say anything at all, then!' These excuses use empathy manipulatively to avoid responsibility and force the person who is holding the narcissist accountable into feeling sorry for them—so sorry that they end up reassuring the narcissist, being sidetracked from the original issue."[10]

In *Truth and Repair: How Trauma Survivors Envision Justice*, Judith T. Herman brings up how many survivors yearn for a genuine apology:

> They want the perpetrators to admit their crimes and take full responsibility, with remorse and without excuses, to recognize the suffering they have caused, and to show that they are willing to do whatever needs to be done to make amends. True apology also offers a promise, implicit or explicit, that the offender has undergone a moral awakening: that he is a changed man and will never repeat his crime. Genuine apologies are personal, they are emotional, and they create the possibility of repairing a relationship.

When the offender humbles himself to beg or pardon, the gesture represents a reversal of the power dynamic between victim and offender. The power to grant or withhold pardon belongs to the victim. Such gestures of humility go a long way to restoring the victim's dignity and self-respect. They assuage feelings of helpless rage and bitterness that torment the victim, and often they call forth spontaneous feelings of forgiveness. Unfortunately, such full and genuine apologies are rare.[11]

Here Herman means an authentic apology: both saying "I'm sorry" and then taking responsibility for what one did, including asking, "Is there anything I can do to make it better?" This is followed by actually making a concerted effort to change one's behavior while also allowing the survivor to heal at their own pace. None of this "I'm sorry, but . . ." followed by whatever excuse, rationale, or reason the perpetrator can concoct to explain away to justify their injurious behavior. This includes shifting blame by saying, "I'm sorry you feel this way," "Mistakes happen, nobody's perfect," or "I wouldn't have done anything to you if you hadn't let it happen," as though the person being abused was somehow responsible for the scenario.

> The very same tools we use to build a better world can also be used against us.
> —Malcolm Gladwell, *Revenge of the Tipping Point*[12]

Hopeful, not Hoodwinked

In reviewing my book *Jesus Died for This?* before its republication by Lake Drive Books in early 2025, I felt my heart sink when I realized the extent to which I'd been hoodwinked. Throughout the book, I referenced those whom I thought were peers and whose work I once praised, who proved to be plastic when they got their shot in the media spotlight. Others showed their narcissistic side in more subtle but equally sickening ways. When I first began to experience such negative energies, I'd pray for the day when we could all come together and rekindle that spiritual spark that once drew me to their work in the first place. But I've learned to stop dreaming. Whenever I'd show up to one of their gatherings, they'd talk and talk and talk about their mission to build a better church, but in the end, it all proved to be a mirage. No amount of wishing can bring back that magic.

In the same spirit, I've given up any hope that those in my life who possess extreme narcissistic characteristics will change. This awareness allows me to forgive them without expecting any connection I thought we once had. Yes, I'd embrace such an authentic change of heart, but I no longer hold out hope for an apology, knowing the odds of such a genuine reconciliation are akin to winning the lottery.

Freed from this empty hope, I can move on in faith. Now that I've disengaged from those energies that once kept me bound, I am finding ways outside of institutionalized Anglicanism to incorporate the virtues inherent to this denomination's three-stooled theology (scripture, tradition, and reason) that remain imprinted on my soul. With the guidance of a few trusted companions, I can now reenter select spiritual spaces in moderation and decide when it's worth staying or when a given situation feels just too toxic for my soul. As I noted at the beginning of this book, I've become a traveling pilgrim in the spirit of my twelfth-great-grandfather Roger Williams. We're both in search of the truth, knowing full well we'll never actually enter our own Camelot. But we know we have to keep on trying.

While Roger went about his mission as a solo seeker, in our current state of global turmoil, I feel called to connect with people at a deeper level and explore what we have in common in our shared humanity.[13] I sense I am not alone in this search, though the question remains—just how do we go about this quest without losing both our souls and our sanity?

> When I look at narcissism through the vulnerability lens, I see the shame-based fear of being ordinary. I see the fear of never feeling extraordinary enough to be noticed, to be lovable, to belong, or to cultivate a sense of purpose.
>
> —Brené Brown, *Daring Greatly: How the Courage to Be Vulnerable Transforms the Way We Live, Love, Parent, and Lead*[14]

As I waddle along my admittedly crooked spiritual journey, academic and author Brené Brown reminds me of the need to extend compassion to those who display narcissistic traits: "What almost no one understands is how every level of severity in this diagnosis is underpinned by shame. This means we don't 'fix it' by cutting people down to size and reminding folks of their inadequacies and smallness. Shame is more likely to be the cause of these behaviors, not the cure."[15] This knowledge serves as a helpful reminder for me to be merciful toward those with a malignant spirit, though I confess some days the best I can do is mumble a "may all be well with this &*^%$#" under my breath. But at least it's a start.

If my B.S. detector beeps when I first meet someone, I pause. This sound signals that I need to be on guard. But instead of immediately labeling anyone who sets me off as a raging malignant narcissist or even a psychopath, I explore why I seem to have difficulty connecting with this person at this moment. Here are some helpful questions I ask when encountering someone who seems to be unable to engage with others beyond the most superficial level:

- Can they express interest in anyone other than themselves?
- Do I get a sense that they want to reach out but seem to lack the ability to make genuine connections with others?

❑ Are they dealing with severe stressors and lacking the emotional bandwidth right now to address anyone else's concerns?

❑ Do they tend to be a creative dreamer who lives in their head at times, thus tuning the rest of the world out?[16]

If the answer is "yes" to any of these questions, then most likely the person doesn't fit the bill for being a full-blown narcissist. Granted, they still may be a Jerk for Jesus or a mindless meditator who might try one's soul at times. (If I'm being totally honest with myself, I have to admit I've fallen into these categories on more than one occasion.) However, over time, I might be able to make at least a superficial connection and possibly even be in community with this person, even if the relationship can be somewhat rocky at times.

Changing Community Culture

According to Scot McKnight and his daughter Laura Barringer, co-authors of *A Church Called TOV*, the number one question they get asked by those in toxic churches is if they should stay or leave. Barringer reflects, "We found that for those who want to stay and make changes and help transform the culture to one of TOV (Hebrew for goodness), the further a person is away from the power circle, the less influence they're going to have to make change. So ask yourself if you are in a position where you can create small TOV circles within a small group that over time can outweigh the toxicity and enable change to truly happen."[17]

John Pavlovitz concurs:

The more influence a singular person or small group of people has, the greater the chances they are going to be negatively altered by that influence or to leverage it to serve themselves. Individual faith communities or denominations that actively resist personality-centered leadership will not be beholden to those individuals because their growth or sustainability will not be tethered to them. Healthy churches should have genuine community and disparate voices at their center, but this takes time and great effort.[18]

In his research, Lance Ford, co-author of *Starfish and the Spirit* and author of *UnLeader*, points to how healing from unhealthy patterns of leadership requires a move toward a system of mutual accountability and submission at the local level: "We have to slay the dragon of power-based titles and positions." While our current celebrity-making culture may focus on making kings, Ford points to the need for a stronger collective of voices where no one is trying to dominate. "From a systemic basis, we need to debunk the groupthink that tells you you're crazy when you speak up. You're not rebelling when you push back against a leadership system that was put upon you and abused you," Ford opines.[19]

In trying to create an actual caring community, Mullen reminds us that sometimes supporting the victim means immediately withdrawing support from those who have yet to speak the truth about the abuse and refuse to allow light to shine: "This might seem harsh or an overreaction, but consider what it communicates to the watching victims when they see people gathering around the people who wounded them—to see them giving money to the institution, using their services, applauding their efforts, and endorsing their legitimacy. Consider also what it communicates to the public. Your participation signals to others that this is a safe place."[20]

Deborah Loyd, pastor and teacher, reminds me how horizontal leadership represents a sign that one is in a healthy community:

A pyramid form of leadership has the narcissistic leaders on the top. When you get to the bottom, you have all these many little people that are serving the pyramid, but they don't know exactly what they're doing. So these people come and go all the time because they get dissatisfied or feel mistreated. But what if you take that pyramid and flip it upside down by putting the leader at the bottom? Then the leader is there to serve those in leadership positions. And in turn, those people are there to serve the people coming and going. When you see a leader asking, "What can I do to help you be successful?" then you've likely got somebody that's on the bottom of this flipped pyramid of leadership.[21]

This brings to mind the work of Thomas Erikson, who suggests that humility might be the opposite of narcissism: "Genuine humility is a great source of strength. The ability to view and assess yourself objectively and exaggerate neither the positives nor the negatives. Truthfully. Correctly, accurately, and precisely."[22] According to Richard Foster, the founder of Renovaré USA, "In a society where raging narcissism dominates the moral landscape, the virtue of humility is often dismissed as irrelevant. Not only is humility vanishing from contemporary culture, but we are also witnessing how destructive a lack of humility has become among our churches and ministry leaders."[23]

In *Humble: Free Yourself from the Traps of a Narcissistic World*, Daryl Van Tongeren notes the difficulty of changing a church's humility. He cites a study he did with some colleagues where they tested an intervention from positive psychology on different church groups. In order for the churches to agree to participate, Van Tongeren had to adopt a design that isn't ideal for social science by letting churches self-select into the humility treatment group or the neutral control group. The humility treatment group had participants work through a sixteen-exercise workbook for four weeks. The researchers obtained ratings of the participants' humility from both the participants and those around them before and after the intervention. Interestingly, when analyzing the study's findings, Van Tongeren found that the self-selection process wasn't sufficient to affect an individual's level of humility, though it did increase the agreement between the target's assessment of their humility and how others assessed them: "Participants did become more accurate in assessing their own humility thanks to the intervention. But sadly, the intervention didn't make them any humbler, in their own eyes or in the eyes of other people."[24]

Given the limited research to date on humility, how do we best proceed? Brad Sargent recommends looking for spiritual communities whose leaders demonstrate the opposite characteristics of those found in toxic leaders. For example: They remain open to questions and concerns from all members instead of trying to lock their followers into a dictated, rigid belief system. Most importantly, the leaders have an accountability system in place that ensures power is distributed equally among all members so that all have a voice in the creation and curation of this community. The members' contributions of their time and talents are respected; no one forces them to give, give, give until they finally burn out. Once burned, the former member finds themselves discarded with the narcissistic minded leader moving on in search of the next over eager disciple, who is all too ready to please.

These practices, which Sargent calls "the redemptive reversal," offer a practical starting point for creating a constructive checklist for safer and sustainable involvement in spiritual communities. Instead of enabling abuse and writing off those impacted as expendable, the focus shifts from defending those in power to empowering and standing in solidarity with survivors of toxic leadership while holding perpetrators accountable for their actions."[25]

Now, I would never advocate for the creation of communities and common ground just so everyone can come together to sing

Kumbaya and ponder our navels in search of some esoteric god-goo, and this can happen even in the spiritual communities Sargent supports. No matter how we create spiritual community in the U.S., our narcissistic tendencies can often issue forth platitudes that might create a false sense of community for those present, but to the rest of the world, we become a Shakespearean mess: "Full of sound and fury, signifying nothing" (*Macbeth*, Act V, Scene 5).

On the rare occasion when spiritual communities issue some kind of an actual resolution, their commentary tends to favor majority rule, thus casting aside those minority viewpoints who find themselves once again on the outside, unable to have a voice at the inner table. Sermons, lectures, protests, and rants often do little to change our minds about a given sociopolitical or theological topic, but the kinds of spaces that truly welcome all enable our hearts to become transformed by being in community with those who differ from us in terms of education, ethnicity, gender identity, sexual orientation, marital status, political affiliation, and other markers that are all too often used to divide us.

Ideally, a non-narcissistic community embodies much of what Christianity once did: local, relational, externally focused, and "neighboring." Over the years I've seen an increasing number of formerly paid or volunteer individuals once connected with the church move into this kind of missional approach, without the institutionalized church as a base.

> Punk used to be yelling and making a big noise, but, now, this is the resistance—kindness and empathy.
>
> —David Byrne[26]

Such a healthy community would be led by those who not only can express empathy and compassion but who also genuinely appreciate the individual contributions of each member. In reflecting on how some of my past friendships have soured, I have to wonder why it is so hard for folks to say phrases like "thank you," "I'm grateful for what you did," and other remarks that indicate one's contributions to the community are acknowledged and appreciated. For example, I'm thinking about a now bestselling expastor for whom I made the connections that enabled their first book to get published. They're now retelling the story as though they did it all by themselves. This news took me a bit by surprise, as we had what I thought was a very fruitful conversation about the challenges facing a newly published author. In fact, they nodded in agreement when I told them my long-standing mantra that keeps me grounded whenever I get any recognition for my work: "There's no point in having street cred unless you use it to help build up the neighborhood."

In hindsight, I can see how in my desire to help new voices such as this person, all too often I fail to recognize how they are creating their personalized Christian castles instead of working with me for the common good. Once they get themselves shown as the latest, greatest king or queen, they focus on promoting their unbiblical brand and abandon the prophetic proclamations that drew me to their work in the first place. Hence, the will of the people remains silenced by both the political and religious institutions that define American Christianity as well as by our secular society as a whole.

This aforementioned incident happened about two decades ago, when I was still in the professional Christian world. At this time there still existed a buzz surrounding progressive Christian authors. Said buzz has well buzzed on, but try to tell that to the institutional church. These god-awful golden children continue to promote themselves as revolutionary religionists even though they all look like aging rockers replaying their favorite hits to an ever-graying audience. It's like watching a Christian version of VH-1's ancient "Where Are They Now?" series.

Of course, those peddling their politicized version of spirituality hope you will buy not only their shtick but also their books, podcasts, and other spiritual swag. As a broke-ass religious satirist and storyteller,

I have been tempted more than once to join them in peddling my wares to the missional masses. After all, such moves made millionaires out of the likes of megachurch pastors Rob Bell, Rick Warren, and Joel Osteen, not to mention the hordes milking the monied mindfulness movement. Setting aside my inability to pen such faith fluff without losing my lunch, I've seen too many instances where a spiritual creative's work that once had the power to transform becomes trivialized when they choose to cash in and capitalize on their craft.

Yes, like most creatives I know, I have taken work that doesn't feed my soul because I needed to secure basic necessities such as food and rent, not to mention the occasional foray to "fund my fun." But I'm referring to the proclivity of those in the spotlight to cash in on their talents by consistently churning out what sells rather than what speaks to their heart. Over time this spiritual spin cycle snuffs out the creative spark that made their original work sing. In my estimation, very few artists can go commercial for more than a bit and reemerge with their integrity and art intact.[27]

During my tenure in the Christian publishing world, fellow like-minded authors promoted each other's works—that's how the Bible biz goes. And yes, I get why many of those I once considered professional peers no longer connect with me. I'm not marketing myself as an explicitly Christian author; hence, I'm not a practical professional contact to help them advance their ability to remain in the media spotlight. Unlike earlier incidents where such narcissistic moves would have triggered me, I've done enough work on myself that I now know not to personalize them. I can step back and see how these people have been appropriating both my and others' work in a quest to build up their progressive platform even as they engage in bullying both online and off. But instead of getting angry and pissy like I did in the past, I find myself feeling compassion for these self-proclaimed Christian celebrities. What's going on with their souls that they feel a need to prop themselves up by denigrating and dismissing others just so they can present themselves to the publishing world as more marketable?

Also, I've learned to spot extreme narcissistic energies when they occur in secular spiritual settings as well. For example, when I reflect on my more recent experiences volunteering my time and talents in the greater Portland area, I see how I at first failed to pick up on the signs that I was surrounded by what I see now were mean girls. Initially I thought I was helping to create new forms of community that would speak to the Celtic spirituality and sacred sexuality that embody the outdoor spirit of the Pacific Northwest. However, during the summer of 2020, the combination of COVID, almost-daily Portland protests that soon focused on virtue-signaling and rioting rather than defending the rights of Black folks, and the ongoing rise of partisan politics produced one heck of a stinky spiritual stew. Those who delighted in this dish insisted that this would be the *only* dish served at their gatherings. The increasing polarization created a two-tier system that divided those who were once in good standing within these communities into worthy/good/righteous versus unworthy/bad/sinful categories.

Those like me who might prefer more inclusive fare that welcomed all soon found ourselves disinvited from those tables where we were once viewed as valued members of the community. Just like with my relationships with fellow Christian authors, it turned out this newfound social/political community was led by those with extreme narcissistic energies, not a robust, healthy sense of relating to others, and this resulted in a short-lived movement.

> You own everything that happened to you. Tell your stories. If people wanted you to write warmly about them, they should have behaved better.
>
> —Anne Lamott, *Bird by Bird: Some Instructions on Writing and Life*[28]

The Joys of Accountability

Even though I love dancing solo, I find my movements tend to be more magical when I pair up with another dancer. Likewise, as you travel in search of communities that feed your soul, perhaps you will surround yourself with a few trusted travel companions. Such souls can help you discern if the spiritual sensation you're feeling is a genuine movement of the spirit or just another round of faith farts. Back in the '80s, I recall hearing the late Australian evangelist John Chapman opine, "Is it God or is it gas?"[29] Answer this question correctly, and your soul and sinuses will thank you.

By the time I launched my first book, *Red and Blue God, Black and Blue Church*, I had been a satirist for over a decade. During this time, I lost count of the number of times I interviewed a promising new voice only to have them become all *American Idol*–ized once they hit the glare of the media spotlight. I knew a similar fate could befall me if I didn't surround myself with those who would be willing and able to tell me whenever I got too full of my own hubris and needed to be brought down to reality.

Over the years, this small circle has changed a bit. A few friends I thought I could trust used our private conversations as a way to garner intel they then dispersed within their allegedly "Christian" circles to raise their street cred by spreading false rumors about me. Unfortunately, I let my anger get the better of me in my quest to fix this scenario, to get justice for those they abused in this process, including myself. I have since learned that the best way to handle communities led by spiritual narcissists is to leave. Understandably, you may crave an apology, but what you'll get will be asinine instead. So just go. Then get whatever help you need so that these energies no longer trigger you. Trust me, I'm not spouting Oprah-esque omens. Rather, I'm simply noting that the more you can fine-tune your awareness of narcissistic energies, the easier it can be to discern who can be a trusted guide on the journey and when to run for the hills. Just as I cured my addiction to Diet Coke and now only drink sodas made with organic ingredients, I know that hanging out with the Christian cool kids or their secular counterparts, the enlightened elites, would prove to be more Instagramable than inspirational.

Today, our states of bondage are not material so much as emotional and psychological and spiritual, and all states of material bondage still existing would disappear in a moment were we to free our hearts and minds. What we most need to be free of now is our tendency to distract ourselves from the pain of the world, our tendency to isolate rather than join with others, our own selfishness and narcissism, and unforgiveness and greed. Those tendencies are not our sins, but our wounds. They are our modern prisons, and the modern version of the American Dream is to break free of these chains within ourselves.

—Marianne Williamson, *Healing the Soul of America*[30]

On his blog, David Hayward, a.k.a. Naked Pastor and author of the book *Flip It Like This*, offers these steps for those seeking to find a healthy spirituality: "Be conscientious about what you eat. Be diligent, independent, and responsible. Read labels. Distrust companies. Do research. Taste test. Same with your spirituality. Taste and see. Test. Discern. Choose wisely. What makes you be and feel your best?"[31]

BE AS CONSCIENTIOUS ABOUT YOUR
SPIRITUALITY AS YOU ARE YOUR FOOD

1. Question the label.
2. Investigate the manufacturer's claims.
3. Study independent research.
4. Examine the contents.
5. Test the effects.   ©nakedpastor

© NakedPastor

As we continue to heal and grow, hopefully we will develop what Dr. Craig Malkin termed in his book *Rethinking Narcissism* "healthy narcissism."[32] While the research into narcissism has evolved since this work was first published in 2016, Malkin's sentiments about the need for us to achieve a healthy sense of self remains valid. Feeling a little special helps us to see ourselves and those we love through rose-colored glasses (though not so cloudy we can't see any major red flags), remain resilient when we fail, feel passionate about what we love, and pursue our dreams even when they seem a bit beyond our reach. Regarding our interests and needs as important enough to let the world fall away and see where our desires take us is an important aspect of being healthy. Armed thus with a stable ego, we can dare to dream and seek out other like-minded souls in a mutual quest to bring our visions to fruition. We will also have enough self-awareness to recognize when a project or community no longer resonates with our souls and it's time for us to live in peace and seek other places to play.

7
Connecting in Community

My search for spiritual communities appears to mirror the reflections in "Believing," a project spearheaded by Lauren Jackson, a *New York Times* associate editor and writer for the paper's newsletter "The Morning." She defines this project as "exploring how people experience religion and spirituality now." In her estimation, "Religion offers people three Bs: beliefs about the world, behaviors to follow, and belonging in a community or culture." According to Jackson, her research is "backed up by a major research study by Harvard and Baylor Universities that affirms what so much other data has shown: People flourish—they live happier, healthier and better lives—if they have strong social connections," adding that "religions, for all their reputational baggage, can provide people with robust communities."[1]

While Jackson focused her research on the role of religion in contemporary society, readers responded to her inquiry by indicating their strong desire to belong to a community in rich, profound, and sustained ways. I agree with her that religion *can* provide these types of connections, but as the reader responses seemed to indicate, folks are finding communities elsewhere. Let's face it. The institutional church has lugged around so much baggage for so long that it's become biblically bowlegged. Self-appointed church thought leaders can proclaim all they want, "If you build a better church, they will come," but the stats I've quoted from PRRI elsewhere in this book tell another story.

So where do we go? Here are some reflections to help get you started on your journey.

Are Brewpubs and Tasting Rooms the Churches of the Future?

They say you never forget your first. I still remember the time when I encountered that holy

© Becky Garrison

trinity of fly-fishing, cigars, and Scotch in the '90s. Lagavulin 16, to be precise. During this time my focus as a writer was still satirizing profits-over-prophecy Christians while doing the occasional straight reporting piece on religion for Christian media outlets or a travel piece penned as part of my ongoing adventures. Over time I shifted my focus away from satire and instead reported on grassroots ventures that helped connect people in our shared humanity.

When this exploration took me from the Northeast to the Pacific Northwest in 2014, I stopped marketing myself as a professional Christian author—something I increasingly saw as shtick. That said, I was still marketing myself as a religion and travel writer.

Due to ever-evolving market trends, I shifted from travel to covering the region's craft culture, with a focus on beer, cider, spirits, and wine, as well as the regional festival scene and the rise of secular spiritual communities. As the market moved overall from writers telling stories to influencers and content creators marketing their wares, I found myself getting triggered, but I couldn't figure out exactly why I was experiencing the same spidey sensations I felt when I was covering Christianity. I now realize I was once again encountering an overabundance of narcissistic behaviors, particularly among those content creators/influencers who cater to the luxury market. Simply put, they choose to crush the competition rather than connect in community.[2] These elite enclaves felt akin to frozen faith I still feel when I walk into most Christian spaces.

Conversely, I discovered a sense of inner peace whenever I found myself engaging with a visionary entrepreneur who was more excited by their product than any press they might garner. The more time I spent chatting with these kind souls over our shared core values of sustainability, spirituality, and community, the less I cared about being excluded from those who wine and whine. High school drama never ends.

My decision to shift from covering the latest trends to highlighting underreported stories enabled me to savor those opportunities when, in Celt-like fashion, I can almost feel this world touch the next as I take in not just the product but the sense of place, as well as the people behind the bottle. When it comes to my coverage of wine, I don't want to just sip the wine but savor the story. And not some Hollywood hyped-up Aviation-fueled PR spin that pretends to play nice. I love to be cherished by Chardonnay, seduced by Syrah, picked up by Pinot . . . . OK, time to cool down a bit. But wine indeed infuses my soul beyond my bones when I can fully embrace the spirituality of the grape as a marriage of the sun and earth instead of just having wine handed to me with a quicky pour.

Once I'm in this spiritual swirl, I then seek out those savoring similar sips. Together we dance and dine to our own tunes, as we continue our connections. Simply put, I've learned to go where I am appreciated and not dwell on who excluded me from their gated grandiosity (though these learnings took quite a while to put into practice).

A good glass of Pinot, a shot of a craft spirit, an organic cider, or a Pacific Northwest IPA while surrounded by a caring community tends to chase away the B.S. blues sung by spiritual narcissists. In particular, when I began sampling this region's American single malt whiskeys, I found myself rekindling my love of Lagavulin, but with a Pacific Northwest twist.

Given my booze-drenched family tree, I took care to be mindful of my alcohol consumption. Especially with Lagavulin 16, I learned how to savor my liquor, not swig it, as was the practice among most of my extended family members. With each sip, I prayed to the peat and found my true salvation in Scotch. Taken neat with perhaps a drop or two of water to open up the flavors, I can almost taste what the Celts called this "thin line" that separates our world from the next. You can truly drink in the spirit of the Pacific Northwest.

I began to see an overlap between the communion and spiritual experiences some people find in church and the human connection and psychological experience I found in these craft pubs and tasting rooms. Could this kind of third place be part of the solution to the human side of the vanishing church? On the website "Project for Public Spaces," Ray Oldenburg describes how the phrase "third spaces" derives from "considering our homes to be the 'first' places in our lives, and our workplaces the 'second.'" He adds how "informal public gathering places lend a public balance to the increased privatization of home life."[3] I would add to this the necessity of these spaces functioning akin to the office water cooler or employee cafeteria for many of us who work remotely at least some of the time.

With my book *Distilled in Washington: A History* (2024), I've made a shift from writing about the Holy Spirit to distilled spirits, a move that saved both my soul and my sanity. How interesting that not only was it a formal shift in topic, but also a change to more substance (and not just controlled substances). As I continue to explore this region's craft culture, I keep meeting other like-minded pilgrims who have found salvation in these spirited communities.

The following establishments are a few examples where I've observed brewpubs and tasting rooms assuming the communal role once held by the institutional church. Here people come together for friendship, sponsor local fundraisers, and engage in other grassroots community-building endeavors. These are taken from the Pacific Northwest where I'm currently based, but you can be sure you can find similar examples near you.

Copperworks Distilling Co. (Seattle and Kenmore, WA)[4]

Jason Parker, the first head brewer for Pike Brewing Company and co-founder of Copperworks Distilling Company, continues with Pike co-founder Charles Finkel's storied history of supporting the greater Seattle area. When asked how their new tasting room in Kenmore, Washington, helps form a community, Parker conveys this anecdote in his Kentucky drawl: "On two occasions, we had people tell me that what's different about this experience is that they can wander from table to table and talk to anyone in the room, as opposed to being a bunch of private individuals dining out at a restaurant. We're giving the community a place to gather and strengthen their community bonds." The Kenmore tasting room's expansive indoor and outdoor spaces can accommodate maker's markets, music nights, and other community gatherings; it also features a full restaurant courtesy of Del La Soil. Every Monday the distillery donates its space to a local nonprofit, club, or community group to raise money and awareness about its mission. For every cocktail they sell, the local group will receive a dollar. Copperworks also encourages these groups to bring in speakers, stakeholder meetings, and festivals with the goal of becoming a central hub for both local producers and the greater Seattle community.

Kristof Farms (Yamhill, OR)[5]

The Kristofs view their farm, wines, and ciders as the springboard to a community and have designed opportunities to create connections. Their Cider & Conversation events are virtual sessions with the Kristof family where the community is encouraged to come with whatever questions they might have for nationally known journalist Nick Kristof, Sheryl WuDunn, or other members of the family. People often hop on the calls and ask questions about wine/cider, what Nick is currently reporting on and sometimes just general questions and discussion points about current events. In addition, the KF Book Club was started out of their team's love for cider, wine, good books, and, of course, community. Initially their book club met online, but it now meets monthly in person at spaces they love in and around Portland. The Kristofs also joined the Carlton Winemaker's Studio, which was founded in 2002 to attract local artisans and serves as a community. Also, they invite guests to tour their family farm and taste their wines by appointment.

Maysara Winery and Momtazi Vineyard (McMinnville, OR)[6]

Since leaving his homeland during the Iranian Revolution in 1982 and eventually landing in Oregon, Moe Momtazi continues to honor the ancient Persian concept of wine as a living spirit that springs from the marriage of the sun and the earth. As exemplars of the American dream, the Momtazi family carries their immigrant experience forward through their efforts to support Lutheran

Community Services Northwest's (LCSNW's) Safe Route Program. Many of the immigrants in this area who are working at farms, restaurants, vineyards, and other local businesses rely on LCSNW to help them access much-needed resources in the Pacific Northwest. Among the Momtazi family's ventures to support LCSNW include producing five hundred cases of wine they named "Immigrant," with a third of the proceeds going to LCSNW. They also host meetings, immigration information sessions, donor happy hours, and cooking classes for this organization. Additionally, they sponsor FIESTA!, an annual fundraising dinner and auction held at their winery that raises awareness and support for LCSNW's programming. In a society where other immigrants working in the wine industry found themselves in ICE custody circa 2025, the future of those like the Momtazis remains unclear, though one can hope this family's positive influence will only continue to grow.[7]

Northwest Community Ciders[8]

In the Pacific Northwest some cideries take local apples and use them to create community-sourced ciders, with the profits often donated to a designated local charity. For example, Seattle Cider partners with City Fruit by using apples harvested within the urban canopy of Seattle that were not fit for donation to local food banks and couldn't be used for City Fruit's CSA program.

Other pieces I've penned along these lines include explorations of how to turn a wine tasting into a spiritual experience and how to create sustainable communities with craft food,[9] with future inquiries in the works.

While penning this book, I became inspired to explore local festivals like Pickathon (described as Summer Camp for the Soul).[10] This event weaves together music, art, and wellness experiences with a focus on sustainability and supporting local producers that generates a connective communal vibe not present at more trendy events that focus on spectacle not spirituality. Even though I ended up attending solo after my companion could not attend, I found myself surrounded by what felt like the tinglings of an actual community that cares.

In my travels, I keep experiencing similar sensations in other settings that focus on connections not cash. Together, let's raise our glasses and celebrate what we have in common. Cheers! (And don't worry, I am not promoting alcoholism. My extended family drank cheap crapola, not craft, and there was nothing communal or celebratory about their debauchery.)

Pink Martini Sing-a-long, The Square PDX, © Becky Garrison[11]

As I connect with other like-minded spiritual souls, I keep discovering varied experiences and expressions of community that go beyond connecting via Zoom, social media, and other online platforms. As grateful as I am for global opportunities for connection, I find I need to reach out and touch someone in person for these burning connections to truly catch fire. For example, I first met Mark Yaconelli (son of the late Mike Yaconelli) back in 2007 at Greenbelt, a U.K. Christian arts festival. We were both working in the professional Christian realm, but since then he's gone on to form The Hearth, a community storytelling hub based in Ashland, Oregon. We connected again in 2022 for a piece I was doing for *OnlySky* about the power of story to create community. As Yaconelli opined, "You get people together who are on different dividing lines. After we hear each other's story, we feel a little more empathy and connection. We feel less alone and better equipped and more grounded to take on the problems that we're all facing right now."[12]

Kurt Neilson's quest to find community following decades of serving as a priest and chaplain reminds me how we can find community at any stage of our lives if we're willing to look outside the conventional boxes of what constitutes it. Here's his story in his own words:

Reading J. R. R. Tolkien's *The Hobbit* and *The Lord of the Rings* in high school had a great deal to do with my seeking ordination as a priest. These stories address universal themes of journey, companionship, sacrifice, and friendship across differences and are set in a world where the struggle against evil is not always successful nor won by the strong. All the while, Tolkien's well-told tales engage archetypal symbols and myths such as dragons, hidden treasure, cursed rings, wizards, and voyages to the Blessed Realm in the West. Good story shapes us and in fact "tells us" as we receive it, and we in turn retell good story as we embody it and bind it to our own stories. Tolkien's tales "told me" into ordination, and since then I have become a persistent fan of well-told fantasy literature. After all, in the end, all good literature is fantasy, no matter how "real" it strives to be!

My son-in-law recognized a stealth nerd when he saw one. A few years ago, he gave me a twenty-sided Dungeons and Dragons (DnD) die, an iconic symbol of the fantasy role-playing game that is enjoying such popularity today. I fought down my 1980s prejudice that DnD was a game for the socially awkward in their parents' basements and placed the die on my bookshelf.

Then this persistent son-in-law gave us all a set of seven polyhedral dice and gathered us for a family DnD session. We still meet more or less monthly, Zooming in my older daughter, who lives out of state. It is a great way to be together and co-create a story as we play, a dance with one another and with the Dungeon Master who plans the encounter with options for choices that the players make.

Beyond our family encounters, I found my tribe, as it were. There is a pub here on the east side of Portland, Oregon, called TPK (a.k.a., "total party kill," which is DnD speak for when an entire party is "killed" in a difficult encounter with a foe). This marvelous place brews DnD-themed craft beer and partners with a restaurant that serves Cuban-inspired food. They fill their upstairs with tables for gaming. As part of their queer-affirming commitment to holding safe space for all in the gaming world, they created their own ongoing DnD campaign called "The Leyfarer Chronicle," to which one can subscribe and play bi-monthly. After a time on the waiting list, I was offered a place with one party of players that had an opening.

I was received very kindly by these people, who showed great patience with me as I am still somewhat new to DnD. I am pretty sure I am older than the group members by a couple of decades, but I have never felt age discrimination. Partisan politics have never come to the table, and we exercise discretion about our personal lives. I have never outed myself to the group as ordained clergy, and I fear that to do so might give rise to discomfort or worse, especially in deep-blue Portland. It would break my heart if their delightful spontaneity were to be somehow dampened by my presence.

For spontaneous it is. Lovers of storytelling, games, and especially role-play, the group unselfconsciously inhabits their characters and infuses them with personality and history. DnD is chiefly a cooperative game as the party works together to solve mysteries and face danger. One gets to know the strengths and vulnerabilities of each player's character. It is true play at a very high level. One can be whatever one chooses to be, and part of the fascination for me is how our characters can represent our aspirational selves, symbolize personal struggles and questions, and explore our shadows. As a player's character grows, acquiring experience and additional abilities, the player grows along with them. Together, all of us co-create a story that is unique, not to be repeated.

I found I longed for an experience of community where I was welcomed as just another player, not a priest who was expected to import skills and a way of being that satisfied the projections and wants of others. I found this community at the gaming table, all the while renewing my old love of mythic story and exploring what these stories have to say to me as I try to make meaning of this late stage of my life. I'm grateful for this unexpected revisiting of my youth and a chance to play once more in stories that, beneath the whimsy and imagination, speak to core concerns of human life at all times and in all places.[13]

Other places where I've noticed people forming in-person organic connections include:

- ❏ Cannabis and psychedelics collectives (especially those led by Indigenous people) gathered around helping others heal using plant-based medicines

❑ Community food banks, clothing swaps, donation drives, Habitat for Humanity builds, music and movie nights, art walks, and neighborhood block parties

❑ Fans with a shared love of a particular team, band, or other form of live entertainment (as long as the love doesn't turn into bloodlust)

❑ Festivals and other happenings, especially at the local and regional levels

❑ Meet-up and discussion groups formed around a shared interest like art appreciation, drumming, or cycling

❑ Self-help support groups (Here I suggest you work with a qualified therapist to help you discern how to safely form friends who like you are healing from past wounds. Otherwise, you run the risk of forming bonds based on your shared pain and not your collective progress.)

❑ And yes, the infrequent church, synagogue, mosque, temple, or other house of worship—no point in throwing the baby out with the bathwater if the community is led by those who genuinely care with compassion

❑ Wherever and whenever two or three are gathered together, kinship can happen

As always, when exploring your options, watch for signs that the group might be just a bit too cult-like. Yes, the "church" of CrossFit, I'm talking about you and your evangelical approach to exercise. Are you a business, a brand, a community, or a cult?[14] Be particularly mindful of those instances where the price of admission to join a particular club or group becomes so prohibitive that you feel you're joining an elite country club and not a truly inclusive community. I'm not knocking the occasional foray into the lap of luxury. If you get the opportunity to have your *White Lotus* moment, sip and savor the sensations. (That is, provided you don't get murdered, of course.)

Just don't buy into the Cinderella myth that these flash-in-the-pan friends will be there should you find yourself unable to pay to play.

While tribes formed around politics and social causes can create an extraordinarily strong community bonding experience, they often create an us versus them polarizing dynamic that prohibits true community forming outside of their partisan tribe. Yes, you may dig their vibe now, but trust me, any group that engages in authoritarian groupthink will bust your bubble and your butt the nanosecond you differ with even one iota of their agenda.

As you search for connections, see what speaks to your heart. Watch out for any red flags, and pause when you sense the group's actions don't match their message. Also, notice the undeniable shift when a group morphs from being a grassroots collective of like-minded souls into forming an LLC or 501(c)(3) nonprofit. Too often the focus moves from celebrating the community to catering to the whims of a select group of leaders. It's that old "follow the money and you'll see what they truly worship" mantra—an oldie but a goodie.

Going for Goodness

In exploring the topic of spiritual narcissism, I bring up my personal stories not to propose a pity party (that I'd refuse to attend anyway) but as examples of how anyone can become impacted by extreme narcissistic energies, especially during periods of isolation. I hope my stories prove that we can not only survive but thrive after overexposure to such sordid souls.

> When you hear the things people have gone through and realize you've gone through the same, it provides an amazing amount of relief. It gives us hope. And I think that's what we're supposed to get from each other. The hope that, maybe, just maybe, we're going to be okay. Maybe.
> —Marc Maron, *Attempting Normal*[15]

My first experience with the Grateful Dead community in July 2023 gave me the sense of hope and relief described by Maron whereby I could finally, truly connect with my narcissistic/alcoholic family.[16] As the music played, I closed my eyes and returned to my preteen state, that period of time when my late father acted more like a priest and a parent than a passed-out puss. In my mind I was able to reconnect with the time in my life when my hippie parents sought to create a better world. I could finally re-experience the love I felt from my family before my parents' alcoholism ran over their idealism and they died from their addictions in the late 1970s.

For the first time in decades, I imagined my late sister and me dancing together with childlike glee, with my brother joining us. In this brief moment in my mind, my sister was no longer depicted as the family beauty, nor was my brother labeled as the golden child— the same label once awarded to my late father. I wasn't the family's loser dreamer. We were just siblings, the music serving to connect us soul to soul. Then I envisioned my late parents joining in the dancing, followed by the rest of my extended family, both living and dead.

Despite the feelings of intimate connection I experienced, I knew I had to keep these images in my mind and not try to reconnect in person with my extended family. Their ongoing radio silence or cryptic replies, even when I reached out with the infrequent email to stay in touch, told me I was still viewed as the family scapegoat. I guess it was easier to blame me for familial funk than actually attempt to clean up their malodorous mess.

Case in point: Two months prior, my younger sister died from her addictive lifestyle. I went low contact with her for the past few decades after realizing that the Garrison golden child and family beauty bonded together over their collective narcissism. Seems they chose to continue the family cycle of scapegoating the family's loser dreamer with both carrying on the family tradition of boozing beyond belief. But as we never had a complete falling out, I thought for certain we would at least inform each other regarding any major developments in our respective lives like marriage or death. Yet even though everyone else related to me was informed of my sister's death, somehow no one bothered to tell me the news. In fact, I only learned she had died after a kind cousin—one of the few non-narcissists/alcoholics in my family tree—sent me a Facebook message: I needed to contact my brother as something was very urgent. When said brother never responded to my email, I began Googling family members to see who might have suffered a major mishap. My sister's name started with A, so I began with her name, and the first hit was her obituary.

This was the final pièce de résistance. My extended family does not care one whit about me, nor will they ever change. This is who they are. Time to move on.

A few sessions with a trusted therapist enabled me to disengage from family toxicity by helping me discern a healthy way to go from low contact to no contact with all my biological relatives, sans the few who reached out to me with empathy and compassion when they learned of how I had been treated. I highly recommend anyone in a comparable situation getting professional help for themselves in lieu of seeking solace in AITA Reddit forums, TikTok trashing, and the like.

As expected, those who happen to share my DNA or are related to me via marriage continue to twist this saga so they can present themselves as caring and compassionate and me as cray-cray. This behavior tends to be particularly pronounced by those who pride themselves on being faithful followers of the Lord. Such is how godly gaslighters roll. The good news is that I can now with an open heart see them as the wounded souls they are instead of becoming filled with rage for how they treated me following my sister's death and the handling of her estate. Yes, I would like the family artifacts my late sister hoarded, but the retrieval of such pieces isn't worth the soul splattering that would ensue. Yes, I feel melancholy at times, especially around the holidays, but I've also developed rituals either by myself or with those I call chosen family. I no longer call those I'm related to biologically "family," in the same way I no longer call those in church and secular settings who displayed a similar lack of empathy and compassion toward me "faithful friends."

In this spirit, I've unfriended, unfollowed, and disengaged from those individuals and spiritual settings that I now see are riddled with a few too many signs of spiritual narcissism. Reentering these spaces would feel akin to playing in a playground littered with shattered glass and poo that sticks to your shoe. Do I miss those sensations I used to experience when I was around these folks, especially when they pulled out their Dr. Jekyll charismatic personas? A tad, especially when I'm going through a bit of a rough patch and could use a good hug, even if that hug comes with some strings I'd have to detangle later. But then I remember that inevitably their inner Mr. Hyde would reemerge, and I'd end up with my soul smashed once again. Best to hug myself when no one from my chosen family is around than seek out the kind of hugs that hurt.

Do I feel any desire to retaliate against them for their failure to display even a smidgen of compassion and empathy toward me? A bit. But I've learned not to act on these impulses as any temporary feeling of relief I might experience for letting my anger fly inevitably will leave me with a hardened heart. We've all had to learn how to rein in our anger given the extent of our disillusionment in our present moment, whether that's in our personal, professional, social, or cultural worlds. Do I get mad or sad when I hear about all the transformative, tantric, and theological experiences advertised on social media, in book announcements, or in the culture at large that once brought me into ecstatic states of bliss? I'd be a robot if I didn't experience any emotions, though these days my feelings tend to be more bittersweet than ballistic.

I choose not to dismiss my past *or* express regrets, for these magical moments proved to be instrumental in shaping me into the person I am today. Yes, I might get the occasional tinge of FOMO (Fear of Missing Out), but overall, my heart no longer feels a tug to connect with those types of settings I thought were love-filled but which proved to be riddled with extreme narcissistic energies. Moving forward, I take comfort in reflecting on Thich Nhat Hanh's wise sayings on impermanence:

> The past is not truly gone; it is still here, and we can touch it. We may have regrets about the past and believe we cannot go back to fix our mistakes. In fact, touching the present moment, we can still touch the pain and the wounds of the past. We may think that those who have passed away are no longer here—our loved ones, family members, ancestors, or friends. But if we know how to touch the present moment deeply, we discover that they are all still there, alive within us, and we can still speak to them.[17]

Over the years, his teachings enabled me to develop a meditative practice that helped me to connect with those who were once an integral part of my life in the safe container of my mind while keeping my physical body and soul safe from the harm I'd inevitably experience if we actually reconnected. Yes, I've experienced enough unexpected moments of reconciliation that I've learned to never say "never," but I'm also realistic, knowing the best I can do is forgive both those who harmed me and myself for any harm I might have done to others along the way. The rest is out of my control.

If everyone practiced this type of spiritual discernment, I'd be out of a job as a religious satirist once and for all. As someone who now focuses her attention on the craft culture of the Pacific Northwest, I'll drink to that.

© Becky Garrison

Cheers! . . . Cin cin! . . . L'chaim! . . . Proost! . . . Salud! . . . Santé! . . . Skål! . . . Let the global celebrations and connections continue.

Appendix A
Spiritual Narcissism Case Study: Unpacking the History Behind Mars Hill Church's Missional Madness[1]

To help understand the impact of an internationally known spiritual leader with extreme narcissistic tendencies—that is, Mark Driscoll—let's explore the history of Seattle-based Mars Hill Church through the lens of spiritual narcissism.[3] To give an idea of the scope of his abuse, the polling website Ranker includes Driscoll in their list of legendary pastors who fell from grace alongside Ted Haggard, Jim Bakker, Bill

© *The Wittenburg Door*[2]

Gothard, Shoko Asahara, Tony Alamo, Bob Coy, Fred Phelps, Dave Reynolds, Doug Phillips, Jimmy Swaggart, Michael Hintz, Robert Tilton, Josh Duggar, and Rory Coyle.[4] In Driscoll's case, his abuse penetrated throughout the entire Mars Hill subculture, with popular pastor and author Dr. Paul Tripp describing this church as "without a doubt, the most abusive, coercive ministry culture I've ever been involved with."[5]

First a bit of backstory about how an Episcopalian like me connected with this evangelical megachurch mania: My Anglican sensibilities and experiences with the charismatic movement within the Episcopal Church in the 1980s led me to explore the emerging church movement happening in the U.K. and Europe. Here I witnessed localized grassroots ventures with a focus on innovative forms of worship that were attracting those for whom church is not in their vocabulary.[6] I penned three books on my discoveries for Church Publishing from 2007 to 2011 in the hopes that these spiritual sparks igniting my Anglican soul might travel across the pond, but their American counterparts seemed to be more attracted to the Coldplay, candles, and other "cool" confections promoted by holy hypocrites, some of whom promoted themselves as leaders of this Christian clique.

In my research as to why institutional church systems continue to choose trash over transformation, I discovered futurist Brad Sargent's meticulous research documenting a long history of abuses within the Emergent Village (EV) echo chamber. According to Sargent, Driscoll and self-proclaimed EV leaders sprang from the Young Leaders Network (YLN) in the 1990s.[7] Almost from the start, YLN morphed into Yelling Loud Narcissists by throwing down their theological smack, with Driscoll cussin' up a Calvinist streak as the more postmodernist posse countered with their deconstructionist drivel. Think of these pastoral punks as the Religious Ramones, replete with a battle of the bands that would rival any rockumentary—though, as is the case with 99.666% of Christian bands, they pale in comparison to their secular counterparts.

After one too many fights, these former friends now turned faithless frenemies split up. Driscoll went on to found Mars Hill Church in Seattle while his former pseudo-progressive peers planted EV. Their theological trash-talking toward each other escalated. Driscoll preached his own brand of cussin' Calvinism as the EV villagers sang their version of Monty Python's "Philosopher's Song" while doing the Derrida dance, flashing their Foucault, and getting ziggy with Žižek. Both camps of missional men claimed they were the ones being victimized for displaying bravery as religious radicals, a la William Wallace from the movie *Braveheart*.

Simply put, these unbiblical blog battles did not represent legitimate debates around differing theologies but overt displays of thuggery. Women tended to be largely absent from these spaces since we lacked the necessary ontological equipment and spiritual stomach required to witness these men flinging their dude dung all over the place. Also lost in this conversation were the whispers about abuses transpiring within both cohorts, especially involving women, people of color, and those in the LGBT community. Talk about double DARVO.

Given that other writers for *The Door* (a.k.a. Doorkeepers) covered Driscoll, I was not intimately familiar with his ministerial mischief. But I decided to catch him in action when I undertook my maiden voyage to the Pacific Northwest in 2008, hoping to see if all dis Driscoll dissing reflected the religious reality on the ground. Here's an adaptation of the experience as I wrote it for *Jesus Died For This? A Satirist's Search for the Risen Christ*.

Mars Hill Mania

Back in 2008, Mars Hill Church represented the missional monster, the Godly Godzilla that had invaded the Seattle area with over seven campuses. It also boasted 4.4 million sermon downloads from the church's website and eight hundred church planters trained internationally during the prior year. Yes, siree, Mark Driscoll had indeed amassed one heck of an evangelical empire.

I decided to check out The Mark Driscoll Show up close and personal. I almost missed Mars Hill Church's Ballard Campus where Driscoll would be preaching in person because I thought the black-and-gray building was a low-rent community college. After I walked by the information booth and small gift stand, I crossed into the auditorium and was handed a program. According to my bulletin, they had loads of fellowship groups and redemption groups to help the fallen pray away their sins. But what about those who come to church hungry and homeless? How come a church this large doesn't even have a drop-in center of sorts for those in need that can provide at least something to eat, and maybe a warm place to rest?

A holier-than-thou version of Avril Lavigne blasted out power pop tunes accompanied by the all-white coed praise band Sons of Thunder. Not-so-funky graphics played on the projector. A wooden cross on the stage almost faded into the beige background.

No latte-loving men with manbuns in this house, no siree: Driscoll embodies the revitalization of muscular Christianity. This Victorian-esque movement began as a revolt against the women-led church that made men soft and continues today through groups such as the Fellowship of Christian Athletes and Promise Keepers. With an emphasis on building up one's body and soul, these men bond together like some kind of spiritual superglue. The women stand off to the side, ready and willing to serve.

Once the crowd was pumped up and primed to praise, the graphic logo "Pray like Jesus" sizzled on the screen. Time for the Biblical BBQ!

Driscoll entered front and center, looking slightly scruffy yet totally relevant in his untucked shirt and jeans with a Bible propped in his hand like a puppet. His sermon taught us how to pray like Jesus in Gethsemane: pray for self, the disciples, and the church. Driscoll rattled off a whole list of sexual sins that require major prayer—sex before marriage, same-sex marriage, divorce. You know, the evangelical big no-nos.

I waited for the real juicy bits I'd seen posted on YouTube—the "I don't respect any pastor I can beat up," or "I blame the wife when her man strays because she let herself go." Instead, he put on his mellow Mark mask, reflecting that "when we talk with other Christians, we need to be gracious, humble, loving. Don't be deceived. Debate, not division."

What the?! I'm not going to witness any of his controversial, un-Christian crapola? C'mon. The very least the cussing pastor could do is cut loose with a couple of swear words.

As quickly as he entered, Driscoll exited. For all his talk about prayer, he never engaged in said act with his congregation. Heck, they didn't have any prayers of the people or any other kind of corporate prayer.

Next, an assistant pastor encouraged us to come forward for Communion. Despite Mars Hill Church's conservative stances, they got a bit progressive by offering both grape juice and wine. We were also served Communion by male and female ushers— nice to see the girls get to do more in Mark Land than minister to their men and clean up poop in the nursery. Still, no one offered any words of scripture, and I wondered how many people connected what they received to the actual Last Supper with Jesus and his twelve disciples.

Yet another pastor came out and gave us some final instructions. He encouraged us to get involved in The City, Mars Hill Church's online network. Those who were church members were encouraged to make their usual offering, but visitors like me weren't pressured into giving. Pastors stood at the front of the church after the service so one could get a piece of prayer if need be.

After we were dismissed, I walked out into the lobby in search of signs of Driscoll. No pastors were present, though I did see several guys with earpieces and black "Mars Hill Security" T-shirts. What's with Pharoah's bouncers? Let's be honest—the "limp-wristed hippies" Driscoll slams might be full of hot air, but I seriously doubt any of them pack heat.

I can see, though, why some might want this spiritual security, so to speak. In today's troubled times, Driscoll presents black-and-white answers to a world cloaked in gray. I've also walked into more than my share of churches where I felt people welcomed my cash but didn't want to care about me. For those who feel lonely and disconnected, Mars Hill Church offers a cup of lukewarm coffee and ready-made community with no immediate pressure to pledge. Even lousy coffee and a handshake could warm one up a little bit.[8]

While The Mark Driscoll Show brought in the Bible bucks, Sargent's research points to how EV never evolved into an actual village but went bankrupt instead. It seems the progressive branch of the Christian Industrial Complex spent its devotional dollars on the "Emergent" brand with only so much to show for it. Book editors, conference organizers, and media outlets moved on in search of the latest biblical B.S. Meanwhile, reports continued to escalate detailing ongoing on- and offline abuses transpiring within the walls of EV and its sordid stepchild, Outlaw Preachers (OP—for those with a more tattooed theology). Rather than address these myriad concerns, the self-proclaimed leaders used their private online network to cyberbully whistleblowers like me for pointing out their unChristian cruelty.

To date, those ensconced within EV's and OP's inner circles who functioned as either perpetrators or enablers have yet to publicly apologize for this cycle of abuses (emphasis on the plural) that points to a much larger systemic problem that went well beyond Jones' extremely messy divorce. Even though much of the research into trauma and narcissism had yet to emerge, I knew well enough not to enter that den of vipers.

In the ensuing years, I've lost track of the number of times I've met someone from the EV/OP clan who approached me in amazement that I presented myself as sane. Some even apologized, either online or in person, for not inviting me to their events. Back in the day, such invitations would have greatly benefitted my career and pocketbook as a struggling journalist, but in hindsight, my experience watching too many peers sell their souls for the spotlight tells me I'm grateful I never cashed out for Christ. Once again, multiple apologies to anyone who was ever at the end of one of my rants as I raged against this malignant machine. Even though I was right, too often I came off as self-righteous.

Meanwhile, psychology professor and author Warren Throckmorton's in-depth reporting on Driscoll's work uncovered acts of plagiarism on a biblical scale. Furthermore, Throckmorton furnished documented proof that Driscoll's *New York Times* bestselling status represented a pay-to-play scheme cooked up by Result Source, a marketing company that conducts "bestseller campaigns" on behalf of authors. In Driscoll's case, their campaign involved Mars Hill Church buying up copies of his book to contrive empty consumer sales numbers, with most of the books finding their home in the church's warehouse. Add to this missional mess multiple instances of Driscoll misusing church funds, abusing his staff, and terrorizing his congregation.[9] Over time, select ex-members began speaking out with blogs like Wenatchee the

Hatchet and Joyful Exiles,[10] chronicling abuses within the Mars Hill network.

Despite this spot-on reporting, Driscoll continued leading the Acts 29 Network he claimed to have founded and increased the number of Mars Hill Church plants. Emphasis here on the word "claimed." Anecdotal reports, now-deleted church planter blogs, and a few current websites like The Gospel Coalition[11] cited David Nicholas as Driscoll's mentor and the co-founder of Acts 29. Instead, Driscoll promoted himself as the sole founder, with no one else in the Christian Industrial Complex bothering to correct this misinformation.

Once Driscoll careened off the Calvinist cliff while driving a charismatic clown car, both he and Nicholas vanished from the Acts 29 website. The site doesn't seem to have a search function, so if Nicholas or Driscoll *are* somewhere in there, they can't easily be found.[12] Most likely shame's not gonna let it shine, not gonna let it shine, not gonna let it shine. It's that ol' "cash over content and character" dealie. I will say, though, that a key problem in covering church-related abuses is that the media tends to only take notice when the pastor is caught with his pants down—literally. Even though Driscoll's teachings on sex veered more toward the pornographic than the pastoral, as far as we know, he did at least keep his trousers on.

The Truth Is Revealed

Fast-forward to 2013: as I began preparing to move from the East Coast to the Pacific Northwest, I received an email that something was amiss at Mars Hill. I began digging around a bit and connected via email with Throckmorton and Wenatchee the Hatchet. Among other helpful input, they guided me away from some self-appointed Driscoll Destroyers who appeared more concerned with using this case to bolster their social media stats than conducting actual investigative research. Most of these people appeared to be victims of church-related abuses who were now using their clout to bully others. Thanks to this dynamic duo (think Batman and Robin but without the car, capes, or cartoonish antics), I began to see a pattern emerging between Mars Hill and EV. For example, in 2007 abuses within both entities came to light only to be squashed by those in leadership. Driscoll replaced his board with yes-men, thus removing any semblance of an accountability structure that could keep his missional mania at bay.

Conversely, EV prided itself on being "leaderless," a stance that allowed its leaders to do as they please, including Tony Jones replacing his legal wife with a "spiritual wife."[13] By the way, a review of the literature on ethical nonmonogamy makes it clear that even in non-traditional sexual relationships, consent remains key.[14] Otherwise, it's cheating. Full Stop. End of Story. This dynamic to protect the leader explains why church abuses don't get exposed.

While only Jones was actually diagnosed as having NPD, those who marketed themselves under the EV/OP brands exhibited similar signs of clinical narcissism. In particular, EV icon and bestselling author Brian McLaren, Jones's pastor and partner Doug Pagitt, and OP founder and son of the infamous televangelists Jim and Tammy Bakker Jay Bakker were instrumental in ensuring Jones remained in the spotlight despite repeated protests from those abused by those connected to this network.[15] Their *Fall from Grace* was *Shameless* indeed.

As I commented in *The Baffler*, "Sex-shaming culture that keeps women silent may be more prevalent in conservative churches; however, one can find a kinder, gentler form of male privilege that favors the abuser over the abused in more seemingly progressive Christian settings. For example, when medical and legal evidence began surfacing around 2008 that Jones was abusing his now ex-wife, leaders connected to this brand immediately jumped to his defense. I reported for *The Humanist*[16] how *New York Times* bestselling authors Rachel Held Evans and Nadia Bolz-Weber chose to stand behind him. Jones gave them both platforms, endorsements, and other accouterments needed for one to become a best-selling author."[17]

Even though EV/OP had already become DOA (Dead on Arrival) in the eyes of the larger Christian Industrial Complex by the time I moved close to Driscoll's backyard, I thought that perhaps there was a story at Mars Hill I could tell. Since Wenatchee the Hatchet preferred to remain anonymous and Throckmorton was teaching at

Grove City College in Pennsylvania, I realized I could provide the most benefit by serving as boots on the ground. So I girded my loins and began attending services at Mars Hill's headquarters in Bellevue, a suburb of Seattle, as well as connecting with both current and ex-church members.

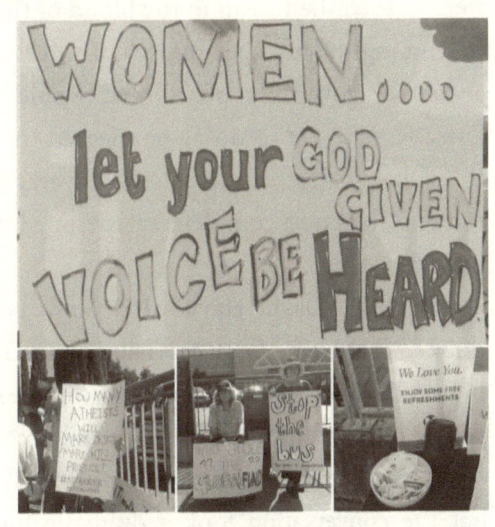

Mars Hill Church protest © Becky Garrison

On August 3, 2014, those connected to Mars Hill and their allies staged a protest that resulted in Driscoll's resignation from Mars Hill and removal from the Acts 29 Network. But instead of actually atoning for his sins and seeking reconciliation with those he harmed, or even just slinking away to spend his ill-gotten gains in private, Driscoll moved to Scottsdale, Arizona, where he reimagined himself as a charismatic charlatan. Back at Mars Hill, Driscoll was a mega-church millionaire, a position he secured through his use of church resources to produce and promote his work, with the monies directed back to Mark and not Mars Hill.[18] But in blinged-out Bible land, Driscoll's multiple LLCs, different trusts, and other missional moves he performed to hide his Mars Hill money paled in comparison to gilded guys and gals who loved their Learjets more than they loved the Lord.

Within this prosperity gospel posse, once a self-appointed spiritual leader claims they are anointed by God, voila, they're in. Hence, any sins Driscoll may have committed while at Mars Hill were now washed clean in the blood of the lamb. Furthermore, by continuing to surround himself with yes-men instead of forming an actual governing board that would hold him accountable, Driscoll was free to do as he pleased, no questions asked. Once Driscoll left Seattle, any media coverage tracking his misdeeds came to an almost complete halt despite former members' multiple pleas for justice.

In 2015, David Hayward wrote a post on NakedPastor.com titled "What Came First, the Thug or the Theology?" where he critiqued Driscoll's defensive analysis of Jones. Hayward argued that people often create and choose a theology that aligns with their personal biases and behaviors. The post itself was relatively harmless, but the conversation took a dramatic turn when Jones's ex-wife joined the comments, sharing her story of abuse involving Jones and the EV community. This sparked over a thousand comments, revealing the darker side of those connected to EV/OP. Due to mounting threats and pressure from various sources, the post was eventually taken down, though archival links of this saga remain online.[19]

Once again, silence left survivors suffering and their perpetrators still preaching.

Christianity Today Disses Driscoll (or Pot, Meet Kettle)

In 2021 *Christianity Today* (CT), the evangelical flagship magazine founded by none other than Billy Graham, released a podcast series entitled *The Rise and Fall of Mars Hill Church*.[20] Those who can't listen to anything Driscoll-related without losing their lunch can get a gist of the scandals documented therein by listening to *The Rise and Fall of Twin Falls*, a gripping five-part mockumentary podcast investigating a scandal involving the Twin Falls' fictional pastor.[21]

True, this series sweeps CT's own sex scandals under the rug[22] and fails to address its own questionable theology and the oversized role this outlet played in elevating select pastors like Driscoll to Christian celebrity status in the first place. But by highlighting other scandals as well, such as the downfall of Hillsong Church, CT at least admitted the larger scope of this problem by noting how fame replaced virtue as the key quality desired in Christian leaders.

Unfortunately, this series did not garner any media mentions outside of conservative evangelical circles. When news broke in 2024 of child molestation charges against Driscoll's mentor Robert Morris, the founder of Gateway Church in Southlake, Texas, I hoped this might generate more interest in covering his protégé.[23] But nada.

© *The Wittenburg Door*[24]

In a similar vein, online social media activists like Baptist Accountability were unable to halt Jones's return to the public stage in 2023 as event organizers for "Theology Beer Camp: The God Pods Strike Back" did the "see no evil, hear no evil, speak no evil" monkey dance.[25] The following year, Bolz-Weber, McLaren, Diana Butler Bass, and other self-proclaimed progressive thought leaders who benefited from promoting their works via the EV platform lent their support to the *Emerged: An Oral History* podcast hosted by Jones and *Homebrewed Christianity* host Tripp Fuller, despite the re-emergence of stories pertaining to past and ongoing abuses committed by Jones and others who built their platform via The EV brand, and to a lesser extent the OP crud.[26]

Furthermore, Jones continued to garner academic respectability via his connections with figures like Ryan Burge of the Danforth Center at Washington University. They collaborated on a project titled "Making Meaning in a Post-Religious America" funded by the Templeton Foundation.[27]

In this faith fracas, Tim Whitaker, creator and facilitator of The New Evangelicals (TNE), emerged as the latest eight-hundred-pound ungodly gorilla to join this progressive Christian circus. As per their website, TNE's stated mission is "to build an empathetic and inclusive space that encourages authentic conversations, connections, and faith."[28] Yet is TNE defying its mission and following the EV unpastoral playbook that pushes a DARVO brand of discipleship? Whitaker himself was instrumental in throwing TNT toward those who questioned Jones's return to the public stage by working behind the scenes with Tripp Fuller on planning the 2023 Theology Beer Camp.[29]

Unlike Mars Hill, where the culture shifted to where those abused by Driscoll were finally believed, the extent of abuses committed by those who benefited from the EV/OP brands remains largely unaddressed. Meanwhile, these deconstructionist dudebros claim faux persecution by their perceived enemies.[30] Conservative or progressive, isn't it all so exhausting to listen to religious ramblers that may talk a good talk but do not apply their words of wisdom to their everyday lives?

Furthermore, why do seemingly respectable institutions like the Templeton Foundation and the Danforth Center support such academic minded abusers? (Emphasis on the phrase "seemingly respectable.") Again, check any individual or organizations' funding streams and mission to see if they're in alignment. For example, there's been some valid criticism of the Templeton Foundation.[31]

The tides may be turning when it comes to these progressive pseudo-punks thanks to a ninety-four-page report issued in 2025 by GRACE (Godly Response to Abuse in the Christian Environment) detailing abuses within TNE network with a focus on Whitaker's behaviors.[32] On April Fool's Day 2025, I received word that William B. Eerdmans Publishing Company had notified TNE they would not be proceeding with the publication of a book that was to be authored by Whitaker.[33]

But all is not lost in TNE land as The New Evangelicals podcast will no doubt make further appearances at future Theology Beer Camps. I guess the organizers decided to ignore the unbiblical bombs Whitaker dropped on those who spoke out when his own abuse was brought to light, with his wife going so far as to defend her spouse using a fake Instagram account.[34] Perhaps some progressive-minded wives are taking a few pages from the conservative church's complementarian playbook by standing by their men a la Tammy Wynette.

In their quest for clicks over content, other content creators/influencers (calling them "authors" is more than a bit of a stretch) continue to team up with organizations like TNE who can give them the platform they need to cash in in lieu of speaking truth to power. Case in point: at the time this book went to press, Christian content creator/podcaster April Ajoy remained supportive of Whitaker,[35] with their joint podcast resuming on April 17, 2025.[36] This move indicates she is continuing with the Rachel 'n' Nadia playbook by supporting the missional males in power over those they've abused, knowing such support will ensure her success within the Christian Industrial Complex. For now, her decision to choose power over prophecy can be considered a success in the short term: Ajoy's publisher, Worthy, continues to pimp her products. Perhaps they should change their name to Worthless, given their cluelessness about #churchtoo abuses coupled with their promotion of Kardashian Christians such as Ajoy. Just a thought.

This defense of self-proclaimed leaders like Whitaker and Jones by Christians like Ajoy, Bolz-Weber, and all the women supporting the Theology Beer Camp crowd may be misguided in the long run. According to the PRRI Census of American Religion conducted in 2013, 35% of men and 29% of women aged eighteen to twenty-nine said they were religiously unaffiliated. Their follow-up survey conducted a decade later found that while the percentage of young men claiming no religious affiliation remained the same, the percentage of young women rose to 40%.[37] Seems a growing number of young adult women can see through this missional machismo and are choosing to invest their time and talents elsewhere.

While conservative evangelicals, who are critiqued by the likes of Ajoy, have a history of protecting theological and institutional hierarchy when stories of spiritual abuse emerge, over at *Baptist News Global,* Pidcock points to his fellow progressive evangelicals doing likewise: "When we carefully examine [the] story about Tim Whitaker and The New Evangelicals, we'll realize the problem isn't that we're going too far in our critique of hierarchy, but that we're not going far enough. We're not recognizing remnants of hierarchy in ourselves and our friends."[38] Sargent adds, "They mentally deconstructed but didn't dynamite the underlying hierarchy, and so they ended up with both hierarchy and hype."[39]

My only question is, is it just hierarchy, or is it also, and perhaps more broadly, a latent narcissism endemic to American culture? Sargent offers this saying he heard often during the '80s recovery movement days: "Same root, different fruit." In his estimation, "Ultimately, it doesn't matter whether they present as conservative or progressive, complementarian or egalitarian; abusive tactics are a common root that shows up in all their fruit."[40]

Some keyboard warriors may appear to be smashing the Christian Industrial Complex to spiritual smithereens, but truth be told, they're simply refashioning this missional media monster into the Deconstruction Industrial Complex. Less missionary but the same misogyny. Furthermore, by meeting mostly online, they manage to hype up their holiness while masking their messiness, and they weaponize their online connections with a storied history of doxing and cyberbullying that demonstrates how they act more infantile than incarnational.

In a November 20, 2024, Zoom interview with Throckmorton, I inquired why he concluded Driscoll was a narcissistic church leader. This was his response:

> The whole church was built around Driscoll and organized around his ego. He would preach in one place, and then his sermons were all broadcast to all these different church plants located across the country. These church plants had pastors, but none of them taught or preached in any significant way. So you had this organism, [Driscoll], at the center of the church with everything geared toward maintaining this system.[41]

This dynamic sounds very similar to the pyramid scheme–style of leadership I observed among the EV/OP posses. Surprise, surprise. When I asked for signs one is encountering a church led by those with extreme spiritual narcissistic tendencies, Throckmorton offered this sage advice: "If the church is more about the minister than the people in the ministry, then that is a red flag. When keeping the pastor happy is the goal instead of serving God and the people, then you have a problem." He added how those coming out of Mars Hill felt it wasn't about spirituality or God at all but rather about making the church, and by default Driscoll, look good.

I would add that another red flag is if a congregation doesn't have any involvement in the church's decisions. Everything moves according to the leadership, and there's no transparency or organizational democracy or especially institutional oversight above these mega-church megalords. Be sure to watch how those in leadership react when you ask to see a budget. If you can't follow the money, odds are it's hidden among the leaders' assets. Also, the closer you get to the leadership, you find that in a church like Mars Hill, the leaders have a sense of entitlement. As Throckmorton observes, "The leaders and those closest to them believe they deserve special treatment and privileges that other people don't. There's a lack of empathy that comes from the leader. As such, those leading the church have difficulty understanding the feelings of those underneath them."

Another key sign is to watch what happens when you say no to a request. Watch how they respond when you say, "I can't do what you're asking me to do." Do they push you aside? Throckmorton adds that most of us can tell when someone tries to manipulate us using spiritual language: "Well, if you were committed to the ministry, then you would do that," or "You didn't share with others what Pastor Mark said last week."

When asked if those who display Driscoll-level signs of spiritual narcissism can be cured, Throckmorton notes how as a mental health matter, narcissism is difficult to treat. "Success requires a long-term commitment to treatment," he says. "As a church matter, I don't recommend staying with narcissistic leaders. You as a church member are not going to be able to fix the situation. There are plenty of churches. Go find another one." As long as pastors like Driscoll could remain on center stage as the main event, Throckmorton says, things might run smoothly. Once something threatens the organism at the center, however, all its defense mechanisms will organize themselves to defeat anyone who is attacking it. "Then when this organism is exposed and people leave, they often look for somebody to take this organism's place," he adds. In the case of Mars Hill, some ex-Mars Hill members gravitated toward that other Mars Hill Church based in Grand Rapids, Michigan.

Wenatchee the Hatchet documented how others who fled from Driscoll's abusive tactics found solace in the liberal equivalent of a cussin', hipster pastor, Nadia Bolz-Weber.[42] In typical narcissistic fashion, both branded badasses reimagined themselves once their Muscular Christianity schtick ran its bestselling course, so to speak. Driscoll went from Calvinistic to charismatic while Bolz-Weber rebranded herself from a spiritual shock jock to yet another Oprah-esque lifestyle coach. Such rebranding without much introspection continues the cycle of abuse while also continuing to attract new adherents unaware of these guru's abusive histories. Thus the Christian cash keeps coming in.

Throckmorton leaves us with this reflection: "Just because they're liberal doesn't mean that they can't have a system like Mars Hill Church. People tend to gravitate toward what they know, and I think that's probably why people leave Mars Hill and then sadly find themselves in similar systems when they look at another church." I couldn't have said it better myself. To paraphrase David Hayward, a.k.a. Naked Pastor, it's the thuggery not the theology that defines an extreme spiritual narcissist.

Appendix B
Resources for Beginning the Healing Journey

I am so grateful that more people are speaking out about the insidiousness of narcissism, there are more support groups, books, and tools that help people find their way toward greater health and freedom after being tangled up with a narcissist, either in a relationship or in an organization.

—Kathy Escobar, author and pastor of The Refuge[1]

Acceleration Resolution Therapy (ART)
https://acceleratedresolutiontherapy.com/therapist-directory
(Note: When pursuing a qualified ART therapist, stick to the therapists listed in this directory.)

The Awakened Brain: The New Science of Spirituality and Our Quest for an Inspired Life
https://www.lisamillerphd.com

Beyond We Have Ruined God
Includes my course "Religious Gaslighting," where I list the basic signs of spiritual narcissism
https://beyondwehaveruinedgod.thinkific.com/courses/
    beyondwehaveruinedgod

Charter for Compassion
An umbrella for people to engage in collaborative partnerships worldwide
https://charterforcompassion.org

Decult: Raising Cult Awareness
A volunteer-run charity focused on building global networks and creating resources to educate those who want to minimize cultic harm
https://decult.net

The Desert Sanctuary's Treasure Trove of Trauma Resources
A list of resources Karl and Laura Forehand gathered on their deconstruction journey to address religious trauma
https://thedesertsanctuary.org/treasure-trove

The Futurist Guy's Field Guides
Brad Sargent's resources for designing holistic social transformation with a systems approach that uses an integrative paradigm, interdisciplinary processes, and intercultural partnerships
https://futuristguysfieldguides.wordpress.com

Gaslighting for God Substack
https://beckygarrison.substack.com

Humble: Free Yourself from the Traps of a Narcissistic World
https://www.darylvantongeren.com

Lake Drive Books
A new independent publisher on topics of faith deconstruction, inclusion, self-help, and other "books to help you heal, grow, and discover"
https://www.lakedrivebooks.com

The Lasting Supper
A safe and supportive community for deconstructing your beliefs and finding your path to spiritual freedom
https://thelastingsupper.com

The Guru Papers: Masks of Authoritarian Power
https://www.joeldiana.com

The New Science of Narcissism
https://www.wkeithcampbell.com

Spirituality & Health: Becky Garrison
Articles on narcissism and trauma
https://www.spiritualityhealth.com/authors/becky-garrison

Tia Leavings: Religious Trauma Resources
https://tialevings.com/religious-trauma-resources-2

Traumatic Narcissism
https://danielshawlcsw.com

Who Do We Choose to Be? Facing Reality, Claiming Leadership, Restoring Sanity
https://margaretwheatley.com

Acknowledgments

When you leave, and you're actually out there, flailing like a new little fish, there are people who catch you. The universe catches you.
—Tia Levings, Shiny Happy People[1]

I wouldn't be a religious satirist if it were not for Mike Yaconelli, who edited my first article for *The Wittenburg Door* ("Beavis & Butthead Are Saved," March/April 1994), and then Robert Darden, who served as my editor until the print version of *The Door* closed in 2007. They taught me the fine art of idol smashing and how to spot the glimpses of light that emerged once a golden calf uttered its last "moo." Thank you, thank you, thank you.

In 1996, I connected with the late Gary Austin, founder of LA-based The Groundlings, who taught me how to breathe life into my work by just "being."[2] What a ride. Damn, I miss him, but can feel his voice every time I sit down to write or chat up my work or work with his widow and my vocal coach Wenndy MacKenzie.

Thanks also to David Morris for both convincing me to return to the religious wrestling ring, as well as believing that this book needed to be out there. In a publishing world dominated more by cash than craft, it's a blessing to find a book publishing company that allows writers the time and space to focus on writing while they tend to the marketing and editing tasks. Very few people are gifted in all three areas, as evidenced by the plethora of books, movies, music, visual art, and other media released based not on the quality of the content but on how many clicks the latest 15-minute "content creator" sensation can generate.

In addition, my thanks go out to the rest of the team David assembled to help make this work shine—managing editor Em Einolander, copy editor Stephanie Eagleson, proofreader Kristin Thiel, audio engineer Andy Pearson, and cover designer Jonathan Sainsbury at 6 × 9 Design.

And to those of you who gave of your time to give me feedback along the way, I remain grateful for your kind assistance, as well as honored to be in the presence of such brave souls. A particular shout out to Megan Benninger, Karl Forehand, Christopher Jones, Anke Richter, Brad Sargent, Eyal Shaham, and Thor.pdx, along with a few others who would prefer to remain anonymous.

Finally, my heart goes out to all of you with the courage to stand up to #churchtoo and #metoo abusers operating in church and other spiritual settings. While your voice may sound small and silent, together we sing with glorious gusto those songs that knit us together and point to the possibility of heaven here on earth.

Notes

Introduction: Spiritual Narcissists Among Us

1. See Warren Cole Smith, "Which Shepherds Are for Sale?" *The Dispatch*, August 3, 2024, https://thedispatch.com/article/which-shepherds-are-for-sale.

2. Becky Garrison, *Roger Wiliams's Little Book of Virtues* (Eugene, OR: Wipf & Stock, 2020), 9–10, 76.

3. Portions of this reflection were posted to Becky Garrison, "Nailin' It to the Church: The Spiritual Narcissism Edition," *Gaslighting for God Substack*, December 31, 2024, https://substack.com/home/post/p-153770826.

4. "Fans of Comedy Will Absolutely Love Reading 27 Lenny Bruce Quotes—Women.com," The Official Website of Lenny Bruce, December 9, 2019, https://lennybruce.org/2019/12/09/fans-of-comedy-will-absolutely-love-reading-27-lenny-bruce-quotes-women-com.

5. Becky Garrison, "Cutting the Cords of Toxic Relationships," *Grok Nation*, February 6, 2017, https://groknation.com/soul/cutting-cord.

6. See Max Weber, *Max Weber on Charismas and Institution Building: Selected Writing* (Chicago: University of Chicago Press, 1968).

7. T. S. Eliot, *The Cocktail Hour* (London: Faber and Faber, Ltd., 1950), 99.

8. Thomas Erikson, *Surrounded by Narcissists: How to Effectively Recognize, Avoid, and Defend Yourself Against Toxic People* (New York: St. Martin's Essentials, 2022), 106.

9. For a few suggestions of somatic therapies, see Becky Garrison, "How to Use EMDR Therapy," *Spirituality & Health*, December 16, 2020, https://www.spiritualityhealth.com/articles/2020/10/16/how-to-use-emdr-therapy; "Brainspotting and Other Therapeutic Approaches," *Spirituality & Health*, https://www.spiritualityhealth.com/brainspotting-and-other-therapeutic-approaches; and "Slowing Down with Emotional Isometrics," *Spirituality & Health*, https://www.spiritualityhealth.com/slowing-down-with-emotional-isometrics.

10. "Julie Roys Doubles Down on Dumb, Defends Her Past Abuse of Lesbian Church Member, Even as She Displays Questionable Journalistic Ethics," *The Anglican Watch*, June 30, 2024, https://www.anglicanwatch.com/julie-roys-doubles-down-on-dumb-defends-her-past-abuse-of-lesbian-church-member-even-as-she-displays-questionable-journalistic-ethics.

11. Henri Nouwen, *In the Name of Jesus: Reflections on Christian Leadership* (Suffolk, VA: Crossroads Publishing Company, 1989), 60.

12. Becky Garrison, "Extreme Narcissism Bingo," *Gaslighting for God Substack*, January 8, 2025, https://beckygarrison.substack.com/p/extreme-narcissism-bingo.

1. What's the Big Deal About Narcissism?

1. See Neil Postman (https://www.britannica.com/biography/Neil-Postman) with a bit of Marshall McLuhan (https://marshallmcluhan.com) thrown in for good measure.

2. See Becky Garrison, "Jesus for Sale," *Killing the Buddha*, August 5, 2010, https://killingthebuddha.com/mag/dispatch/jesus-for-sale.

3. _____, "Jerry Jenkins Interview," *The Wittenburg Door*, No. 198, March/April 2005.

4. This email was in response to this article: Becky Garrison, "Paying the Price: Dr. Fred Takes Manhattan," TheWittenburgDoor.com, December 2006.

5. See Warren Throckmorton's work on Eric Metaxas, https://wthrockmorton.com/?s=Metaxas.

6. See Jay Michaelson, "The $1-Billion-a-Year Right-Wing Conspiracy You Haven't Heard Of," *The Daily Beast*, September 25, 2014, https://www.thedailybeast.com/the-dollar1-billion-a-year-right-wing-conspiracy-you-havent-heard-of.

7. Merrill Markoe, "Enough About You: My Explanation of Narcissism," Still Looking for the Joke, December 20, 2023, https://merrillmarkoe.substack.com/p/enough-about-you-my-explanation-of.

8. Becky Garrison, *Jesus Died for This? A Satirist's Search For the Risen Christ* (Grand Rapids, MI: Lake Drive Books, re-release 2025), 131–132.

9. "Gaslighting," Merriam-Webster.com, https://www.merriam-webster.com/dictionary/gaslighting.

10. Becky Garrison, "What Is Gaslighting?" *Spirituality & Health*, https://www.spiritualityhealth.com/what-is-gaslighting.

11. Ramani Durvasula, *It's Not You: Identifying and Healing from Narcissistic People* (New York: Penguin Random House, 2024), 46–47.

12. "Scapegoat," Merriam-Webster.com, https://www.merriam-webster.com/dictionary/scapegoat.

13. Neel Burton, "The Psychology of Scapegoating," *Psychology Today*, June 22, 2024, https://www.psychologytoday.com/us/blog/hide-and-seek/201312/the-psychology-of-scapegoating.

14. See *Surrounded by Narcissists*, 101–103.

15. Portions of this reflection were originally posted at Becky Garrison, "How to Stop Enabling a Narcissist," *Spirituality & Health*, https://www.spiritualityhealth.com/how-to-stop-enabling-a-narcissist.

16. Garrison, *Jesus Died for This?* 125–135.

17. "Narcissism," *Psychology Today*, accessed October 20, 2025, https://www.psychologytoday.com/us/basics/narcissism.

18. Durvasula, *It's Not You*, 15.

19. Oprah Winfrey's Commencement Address, My Wellesley, May 30, 1997, https://www1.wellesley.edu/events/commencement/archives/1997commencement/commencementaddress.

20. Julie Hall, *The Narcissist in Your Life: Recognizing the Patterns and Learning to Break Free* (New York: Hatchette Book Group, 2019), 55.

21. Ibid., 23.

22. Nicole Arzt, "What Is Narcissistic Collapse," ChoosingTherapy.com, May 9, 2023, https://www.choosingtherapy.com/narcissistic-collapse.

23. Sandy Hotchkiss, *Why Is It Always About You? The Seven Deadly Sins of Narcissism* (New York: The Free Press, 2003), 9.

24. Ibid.

25. Hall, *The Narcissist in Your Life*, 54.

26. Matthew Remski, *Surviving Modern Yoga: Cult Dynamics, Charismatic Leaders, and What Survivors Can Teach Us* (Berkeley, CA: North Atlantic Books, 2024), 188.

27. Eve Rickert and Andrea Zanin, *More Than Two: Cultivating Nonmonogamous Relationships with Kindness and Integrity* (Victoria, BC: Thornapple Press, second edition, 2024), 69.

28. Hotchkiss, *Why Is It Always About You?*, xv.

29. Margaret Wheatley, *Who Do We Choose to Be? Facing Reality, Claiming Leadership, Restoring Sanity* (Oakland, CA: Berrett-Koehler Publishers, 2017), 299–304.
30. Ibid., 61.
31. Alexander Lowen, *Narcissism: Denial of the True Self* (New York: Touchstone, 1985), ix.
32. Becky Garrison, "Steve Allen Interview," *The Door*, No. 152, March/April 1997.
33. Jean W. Twenge and W. Keith Campbell, *The Narcissism Epidemic: Living in the Age of Entitlement* (New York: Simon and Schuster, 2009), 245.

2. Prey Not Pray: Unpacking the Unspiritual Dimensions of Narcissism

1. See Matt Kelley, "What Is Satanic Panic? Debunked '80s Conspiracy Theory Is Making a Return," *Newsweek*, July 27, 2022, https://www.newsweek.com/what-satanic-panic-debunked-80s-conspiracy-theory-making-return-1728190.
2. "Spirituality or Ego? What Is Spiritual Narcissism and How to Spot a Spiritual Narcissist," Themindsjournal.com, https://themindsjournal.com/what-is-spiritual-narcissism.
3. John Welwood, *Toward a Psychology of Awakening: Buddhism, Psychotherapy, and the Path of Personal and Spiritual Transformation* (Boulder, CO: Shambhala Publications 2002), 5.
4. Suzanne Degges-White, "Spiritual Narcissists: 12 Signs & How to Deal with One," Choosing Therapy.com, https://www.choosingtherapy.com/spiritual-narcissists.
5. See The Austin Lounge Lizards, https://austinloungelizards.com. A curated playlist of all songs referenced in this book can be found here: Becky Garrison, "A Spotify Playlist for *Gaslighting for God,*" *Gaslighting for God Substack*, April 9, 2025, https://beckygarrison.substack.com/p/spotify-playlist-for-gaslighting.
6. *The Door*, Issue No. 164, May/June 1999, graphic courtesy of wittenburgdoor.com.
7. See "Rob Bell's DeVos Connection," Becky Garrison YouTube Channel, May, 23, 2017, https://www.youtube.com/watch?v=e4l7RDnoio0.
8. Becky Garrison, "Top Ten Signs Your Church 'Might' Be Led by a Spiritual Narcissist," *Gaslighting for God Substack*, January 29, 2025, https://beckygarrison.substack.com/p/top-ten-signs-your-church-might-be.
9. "Narcissistic Personality Disorder," The Cleveland Clinic, https://my.clevelandclinic.org/health/diseases/9742-narcissistic-personality-disorder.
10. See Kelly Clay, "The Top 10 Jobs That Attract Psychopaths," Forbes.com, January 5, 2013, https://www.forbes.com/sites/kellyclay/2013/01/05/the-top-10-jobs-that-attract-psychopaths/?sh=4d2388dc4d80.
11. Remski, *Surviving Modern Yoga*, 217.
12. Julie Roys, "Study Claiming 31% of Pastors Have Clinical Narcissism Is Debunked by Expert Researchers," JulieRoys.com, August 1, 2019, https://julieroys.com/study-claiming-31-of-pastors-have-clinical-narcissism-is-debunked-by-expert-researchers.
13. Brad Sargent, video interview, December 4, 2024.
14. "What Is Love Bombing?" The Cleveland Clinic, February 1, 2023, https://health.clevelandclinic.org/love-bombing.
15. Christopher D. Wallis, *Near Enemies of the Truth: Avoid the Pitfalls of the Spiritual Life and Become Radically Free* (Los Angeles, Wonderwell, 2023), Location 99, Kindle version.
16. Beth Schwartz, email July 31, 2025; "The Impact of Adverse Religious Experiences on Holistic Health: Implications for Patients and Providers," February 25, 2025, https://spiritualityandhealth.duke.edu/files/2025/02/Duke-PDF-2025.pdf.
17. John Pavlovitz, email interview, March 28, 2022; https://johnpavlovitz.com.
18. Becky Garrison, "A Conversation about Religious Trauma with Karl and Laura Forehand," *Gaslighting for God Substack*, February 19, 2025, https://beckygarrison.substack.com/p/a-conversation-about-religious-trauma.

19. Dave Johnson and Jeff VanVonderen, *The Subtle Power of Spiritual Abuse* (Ada, MI: Bethany House Publishing, 2005), 32.

20. Sumeet Singh, Arun K. Yadav, Vinay S. Chauhan, and Mohit Agrawal, "Religious Trauma Syndrome: The Futile Fate of Faith," *Industrial Psychiatry Journal*, August 2024, 309–310, https://journals.lww.com/inpj/fulltext/2024/33001/religious_trauma_syndrome__the_futile_fate_of.65.aspx.

21. Michael J. Kruger, *Bully Pulpit: Confronting the Problem of Spiritual Abuse in the Church* (Grand Rapids, MI: Zondervan, 2022), 8.

22. Wade Mullen, *Something's Not Right: Decoding the Hidden Tactics of Abuse—and Freeing Yourself from Its Power* (Carol Stream, IL: Tyndale House Publishers, 2020), 32.

23. Connie Baker, *Traumatized by Religious Abuse: Courage, Hope and Freedom for Survivors* (Eugene, OR; Luminare Press, 2019), 27.

24. See Ibid., 93–111.

25. See "Trauma Bonding: What It Is and How to Cope," Healthline.com, https://www.healthline.com/health/mental-health/trauma-bonding.

26. Stephanie Moulton, *Healing from Toxic Relationships: 10 Essential Steps to Recover from Gaslighting, Narcissism, and Emotional Abuse* (New York: Balance Books, 2022), 19.

27. Ibid., 18.

28. Durvasula, *It's Not You*, 233.

29. Chuck DeGroat, *When Narcissism Comes to Church: Healing Your Community from Emotional and Spiritual Abuse* (Lisle, IL. IVP, 2020), 23.

30. Lena Derhally, *The Facebook Narcissist: How to Identify and Protect Yourself and Your Loved Ones* (Deerfield Beach, FL: Health Communications, Inc., 2022), 41.

31. Ibid., 33.

32. Moulton, *Healing from Toxic Relationships*, 21.

33. Karl Forehand, J. D. Forehand, Stuart Delony, with guest Megan Benninger, "Tim Whitaker & TNE—How We Enable Abusers," Episode 22, *The Unlearning Curve Podcast*, https://open.spotify.com/episode/1boatMBUBRxjWqVJ8SHiA2.

34. DeGroat, *When Narcissism Comes to Church*, 23.

35. Daniel Shaw, *Traumatic Narcissism: Relational Systems of Subjugation* (New York: Routledge, 2013), xv.

36. _____, "The Role of Shame in Cults, from Recruitment to Recovery," *Psychoanalytic Dialogues* 33, no. 6 (2023): 779–95, https://doi.org/10.1080/10481885.2023.2263056.

37. Shaw, *Traumatic Narcissism*, 49.

38. Ibid., 49–50.

39. *The Door*, November/December 1997, Issue No. 156, graphic courtesy of wittenburgdoor.com.

40. Becky Garrison, "#ChurchToo Comes to the Anglican Communion," *Women in Theology*, August 25, 2025, https://womenintheology.org/2025/08/25/churchtoo-comes-to-the-anglican-communion.

41. _____, "Quiz: Are You a Spiritual Narcissist," *Gaslighting for God Substack*, January 22, 2025, https://beckygarrison.substack.com/p/quiz-are-you-a-spiritual-narcissist.

42. Ranker TV, "The 33 Best Cult Documentaries, Ranked," Ranker.com, February 20, 2025, https://www.ranker.com/list/best-cult-documentary-series/ranker-tv.

3. Identifying the Types of Spiritual Narcissists

1. Marko Marina, Ph.D., "Christian Denominations: A List of All 46 Types of Christianity," Bartehrman.com, https://www.bartehrman.com/christian-denominations.

2. W. Keith Campbell, *The New Science of Narcissism: Understanding One of the Greatest Psychological Challenges of Our Time—and What You Can Do About It* (Louisville, CO: Sounds True, 2020), 10.

3. Brad Sargent, *Futurist Guy's Field Guides*, https://futuristguysfieldguides.wordpress.com.

4. Deven Green, "Betty Bowers," https://www.devengreen.com/betty-bowers.

5. Becky Garrison, "How to Identify a Victim Narcissist," *Spirituality & Health*, https://www.spiritualityhealth.com/identify-a-victim-narcissist.

6. See Joshua Haigh, "What's the Science Behind The Goop Lab's Claims?" BBC.com, February 7, 2020, https://www.bbc.com/news/health-51312438.

7. Becky Garrison, "How to Use Gray Rock," *Spirituality & Health*, March 28, 2020, https://www.spiritualityhealth.com/articles/2020/10/28/how-to-use-gray-rock.

8. _____, "Which Spiritual Gathering Is Right for You?" *Gaslighting for God Substack*, February 26, 2025, https://beckygarrison.substack.com/p/which-spiritual-gathering-is-right.

4. Leaving Christianity?

1. Elise Heerde, *Holy Hell: Saved So Hard I Needed Therapy* (Seattle, WA: Kindle Direct Publishing, 2025), 78.

2. Amanda Marcotte, "#WeToo?" *The Humanist*, April 26, 2018, https://thehumanist.com/magazine/may-june-2018/features/wetoo.

3. Greg Epstein, "Book Excerpt: Good Without God," *The Humanist*, October 13, 2009, https://thehumanist.com/magazine/november-december-2009/magazine_article/good-without-god.

4. See *Roger Williams's Little Book of Virtues*, 9–10, 70–85.

5. "Religious Change in America," PRRI.org, March 27, 2024, https://www.prri.org/research/religious-change-in-america.

6. Derek Beres, Matthew Remski, and Julian Walker, *Conspirituality: How New Age Conspiracy Theories Became a Health Threat* (New York: Public Affairs), 287.

5. Enlightened Energies or Predatory Posing?

1. Commission inquiries at Mayatoons.bsky.social.

2. Joel Kramer and Diana Alstad, *The Guru Papers: Masks of Authoritarian Power* (New York: Atlantic Books, 1993), 31.

3. Shari Das, "Celebrity Therapist Marisa Peer Makes Millions from 'Dangerous' Therapy," *The Times*, May 2, 2021, https://www.thetimes.com/sport/football/article/celebrity-therapist-is-exploiting-the-desperate-k00xlf2cc.

4. See Mustika Hapsoro, "Thai Yoga School Reopens After Sex Assault Scandal," *Vice*, January 28, 2019, https://www.vice.com/en/article/agama-yoga-reopens-sex-assault-scandal; Richard Goodwin, "'He Said He Could Do What He Wanted': The Scandal That Rocked Bikram Yoga," *The Guardian*, February 18, 2017, https://www.theguardian.com/lifeandstyle/2017/feb/18/bikram-hot-yoga-scandal-choudhury-what-he-wanted; Anya Kamenetz, "'We All Have Predators Inside Us,' Can a Neo-Tantric Sex Group Dedicated to Exploring Dark Desires Root Out Abuse?" *New York Magazine*, February 28, 2025. https://www.thecut.com/article/the-neo-tantric-sex-group-that-promised-to-change.html; Jennifer Davis-Flynn, "A New Report Details Decades of Abuse at the Hands of Yogi Bhajan," *Yoga Journal*, January 20, 2025, https://www.yogajournal.com/yoga-101/types-of-yoga/kundalini/abuse-in-kundalini-yoga; "Tantra," *Guru Magazine*, https://www.gurumag.com/tag/tantra; Lauren Crane, "How NXIVM Seduced Hollywood Stars and America's Most Powerful Elite into a Barbaric 'Sex Cult,'" *Esquire*, October 17, 2022, https://www.esquire.com/entertainment/tv/a33658764/what-is-nxivm-sex-cult-celebrities-stars-the-vow-hbo-true-story;   Becky

Garrison,"OneTaste: Female Empowerment or Forced Labor?," *OnlySky*, September 1, 2025, https://onlys.ky/onetaste-female-empowerment-or-forced-labor; and Stephanie Russell-Kraft, "The Survivor Who Broke the Shambhala Sexual Assault Story," *Columbia Journal Review*, May 7, 2019, https://www.cjr.org/the_profile/shambhala-buddhist-project-sunshine.php.

5. For a more in-depth analysis of the history of spiritual leaders both past and present, check out George Feuerstein, *Holy Madness: The Shock Tactics and Radical Teachings of Crazy-Wise Adepts, Holy Fools and Rascal Gurus* (New York: Penguin Publishing Group, revised edition, 1992).

6. Becky Garrison, "Top Signs Your Spiritual Guru is a Spiritual SOB," *Gaslighting for God Substack*, April 16, 2025, https://beckygarrison.substack.com/p/top-signs-your-spiritual-guru-is.

7. Kramer and Alstad, *The Guru Papers*, 33.

8. Ibid., 65, 107.

9. "About ISTA," ISTA, https://ista.life/about/ista.

10. "ISTA Community," ISTA, https://ista.life/community.

11. See IRS.gov, "International School of Temple Arts," (Sedona, AZ), EIN: 61-1888116.

12. Becky Garrison, "Is ISTA a Sacred Sexual Community or a Cult," Medium.com, November 1, 2022, https://medium.com/@becky_garrison/international-school-for-temple-arts-sacred-sexual-community-or-cult-20f29d93b752.

13. _____, "Questioning a Shamanic Love Camp at Auschwitz," Medium.com, January 23, 2023, https://medium.com/@becky_garrison/questioning-a-shamanic-love-camp-at-auschwitz-5f4e42cae15e.

14. Ibid.

15. "ISTA Responds: Accusations That ISTA Performs Animal Sacrifice Rituals," ISTA, November 18, 2024, https://ista.life/ista-responds/accusations-that-ista-performs-animal-sacrifice-rituals-at-its-trainings.

16. Ibid.

17. See Becky Garrison, "Bringing Sacred Sexual Abuses within the ISTA Network to Light," *Gaslighting for God Substack*, March 3, 2025, https://beckygarrison.substack.com/p/bringing-sacred-sexual-abuses-within.

18. "ISTA Update—Communication for Our Community and the Public," ISTA, August 6, 2022, https://ista.life/announcements/announcement-dear-community.

19. 3SC, https://3sc.community.

20. "A Conscious Completion: A Joint Message from ISTA and Baba Dez Nichols," ISTA, May 6, 2025, https://ista.life/announcements/a-conscious-completion-ista-and-dez.

21. "ISTA Responds to an Article in NY Magazine Titled 'We All Have Predators Inside of Us,'" ISTA, March 6, 2025, https://ista.life/ista-responds/ista-responds-to-an-article-in-ny-magazine.

22 Garrison, "OneTaste."

23. See Becky Garrison, "How Tantra Connects Sexuality with Spirituality," *Spirituality & Health*, https://www.spiritualityhealth.com/how-tantra-connects-sexuality-and-spirituality.

24. Gwenn Cody, www.gwenncody.com.

25. Becky Garrison, "Enhance Your Sex Life With a Spiritual Guide," Medium.com, September 22, 2022, https://medium.com/@becky_garrison/enhance-your-sex-life-with-a-sexual-guide-e0e1590f961e.

26. _____, "Selecting a Sexual Guide Who Heals Not Harms," *Gaslighting for God Substack*, May 28, 2025, https://beckygarrison.substack.com/p/selecting-a-sexual-guide-who-heals.

27. "The Acronym," Centre for Sexuality, https://www.centreforsexuality.ca/learning-centre/the-acronym.
28. "Assisted Feedback to ISTA," Safe-Mediation.com, https://www.safe-mediation.com/ista.
29. "Exploring Deeper," https://www.exploringdeeper.com.
30. "Red Flags in Workshops," https://redflagsinworkshops.com.
31. Those wishing to delve into this topic further can check out "Tantra Illuminated," https://www.tantrailluminated.org.
32. J. W. Ocker, *Cult Following: The Extreme Sects That Capture Our Imaginations—and Take Over Our Lives* (Philadelphia, PA: Quirk Books, 2024), 10.
33. Nate Scharping, "Are You in a Cult? Here's How Celebrity Leaders Can Manipulate Their Followers," *BBC Science Focus*, December 22, 2024, https://www.sciencefocus.com/wellbeing/cult-leader-psychology.
34. "Machiavellianism," Britannica.com, https://www.britannica.com/science/Machiavellianism.
35. Anke Richter, https://ankerichter.net.
36. Charlie Lewis, "'There's No Going Back': A Survivor's Story of a Cult's Manipulation and Exploitation," *Crikey*, September 27, 2024, https://www.crikey.com.au/2024/09/27/cult-misa-survivor-story.
37. Anke Richter, "Bert's Labyrinth," *North & South*, September 2015, https://northandsouth.co.nz/2021/05/20/centrepoint-bert-potter.
38. _____, "The Accidental Cult Tourist," *The Echo*, August 4, 2023, https://www.echo.net.au/2023/08/the-accidental-cult-tourist; "My Weekend at OneTaste, the 'Sex Cult' Made Famous By Netflix's Orgasm Inc," *The Spinoff*, November 12, 2022, https://thespinoff.co.nz/pop-culture/12-11-2022/my-weekend-at-onetaste-the-sex-cult-made-famous-by-netflixs-orgasm-inc.; The New Tantra, https://thenewtantra.com; Anke Richter, "Journalist Anke Richter Goes Inside the Cult of Netflix's *Wild Wild Country*," *Stuff*, June 9, 2018, https://www.stuff.co.nz/entertainment/tv-radio/104522551/journalist-anke-richter-goes-inside-the-cult-of-netflixs-wild-wild-country; "Kiwis Speak About Yoga Leader, Swami Vivekananda Saraswati, at Thailand Yoga Retreat Agama," *The New Zealand Herald*, September 15, 2018, https://www.nzherald.co.nz/nz/kiwis-speak-about-yoga-leader-swami-vivekananda-saraswati-at-thailand-yoga-retreat-agama/CQRIYXKBMGR66E6NXFM6G6JC3E/.
39. _____, "Departures," *New Zealand Geographic*, Issue 155, January-February 2019, https://www.nzgeo.com/stories/departures.
40. _____, "Gloriavale Report: Have We learned Nothing From Centrepoint?" *The Spinoff*, March 30, 2017, https://thespinoff.co.nz/society/30-03-2017/gloriavale-report-have-we-learned-nothing-from-centrepoint.
41. John Hunter, https://johnhunterphd.com.
42. Anke Richter, "Centrepoint: Neither Free nor Loving," *RNZ*, May 31, 2021, https://www.rnz.co.nz/news/on-the-inside/443755/centrepoint-neither-free-or-loving.
43. See Sarito Carroll, *In the Shadow of Enlightenment: A Girl's Journey through the Osho Rajneesh Cult* (Boulder, CO: Heroine Publishing, LLC, 2024).
44. "Sannyasin," *Yogapedia*, December 23, 2023, https://www.yogapedia.com/definition/5348/sannyasin.
45. Associated Press in Paris, "Tantric Yoga Guru Gregorian Bivolaru Charged with Human Trafficking," *The Guardian*, November 28, 2023, https://www.theguardian.com/world/2023/nov/28/tantric-yoga-guru-gregorian-bivolaru-charged-with-human-trafficking.
46. Centrepoint Restoration Project, https://www.centrepointrestorationproject.com.

47. *The Door Magazine*, March/April 2000, Issue No. 169, graphic courtesy of wittenburg-door.com.

48. Amanda Montell, *Cultish: The Language of Fanaticism* (New York: Harper, 2021), 12.

6. Breaking the Cycle: Goodness, Not Gaslighting

1. Anne Lamott, *Traveling Mercies: Some Thoughts on Faith* (New York: Anchor Books, 2000), 107.

2. Campbell, *The New Science of Narcissism*, 253.

3. Lisa Miller, *The Awakened Brain: The New Science of Spirituality and Our Quest for an Inspired Life* (New York: Random House, 2021), 7–8. Portions of these reflections were reposted at Becky Garrison, "Are We at the End of a Narcissism Epidemic?" *OnlySky*, April 3, 2025, https://onlys.ky/are-we-at-the-end-of-a-narcissism-epidemic.

4. Kurt Neilson, email correspondence, March 23, 2025.

5. Brad Sargent, email correspondence, March 22, 2025.

6. Jill Leigh, email correspondence, April 18, 2025, https://energyhealinginstitute.org.

7. Tim Minchin, *You Don't Have to Have a Dream: Advice for the Incrementally Ambitious* (New York: Penguin, 2025), 4.

8. Chögyam Trungpa, *Cutting Through Spiritual Materialism* (Boston, MA: Shambhala Publications, 1973), 3.

9. Russell-Kraft, "The Survivor."

10. Helen Villiers and Katie McKenna, *You're Not the Problem: The Impact of Narcissism and Emotional Abuse and How to Heal* (New York: Balance, 2024), 111.

11. Judith T. Herman, *Truth and Repair: How Trauma Survivors Envision Justice* (New York: Basic Books, 2023), 82.

12. Malcolm Gladwell, *Revenge of the Tipping Point* (New York: Back Bay Books, 2025), 8.

13. See Becky Garrison, "Roger and Me and the Quest for Spiritual Freedom," *Reflections*, Yale Divinity School (Fall 2024), https://reflections.yale.edu/article/listening-heart-can-we-temper-polarization/roger-and-me-and-quest-spiritual-freedom.

14. Brené Brown, *Daring Greatly: How the Courage to Be Vulnerable Transforms the Way We Live, Love, Parent, and Lead* (New York: Avery Books, 2021), 22.

15. Ibid., 21.

16. Becky Garrison, "Are You Overusing the Word Narcissist?" *Spirituality & Health*, https://www.spiritualityhealth.com/overusing-the-term-narcissist.

17. Laura Barringer, email correspondence, February 2, 2022; https://www.churchcalledtov.org.

18. Pavlovitz, email interview.

19. Lance Ford, email correspondence, August 31, 2024.

20. Mullen, *Something's Not Right*, 181.

21. Deborah Loyd, telephone call, December 12, 2024.

22. Erickson, *Surrounded by Narcissists*, 268.

23. Renovaré USA, https://renovare.org/books/learning-humility.

24. Daryl Van Tongeren, *Humble: Free Yourself from the Traps of a Narcissistic World* (New York: The Experiment, 2023), 237.

25. Becky Garrison, "Exploring Narcissistic Traits Among Christian Leaders," *Women in Theology*, January 9, 2019, https://womenintheology.org/2024/01/09/exploring-narcissistic-traits-among-christian-leaders.

26. Jonathan Dean, "David Byrne at 73: I Found Happiness in Music and Life After Talking Heads," *The Times*, August 16, 2025, https://www.thetimes.com/culture/music/article/david-byrne-interview-talking-heads-blx0f8rgg.

27. An earlier version of my reflections on the commercialization of craft can be found in Garrison, *Roger Williams's Little Book of Virtues*, 77–79.

28. Anne Lamott, "12 Things I Know for Sure: Anne Lamott Speaks at TED2017," TED.com, April 28, 2017, https://blog.ted.com/12-things-i-know-for-sure-anne-lamott-at-ted2017.
29. John Chapman, https://encministries.org.au/ministry/john-chapman-foundation.
30. Marianne Williamson, *Healing the Soul of America* (New York: Simon & Schuster, 20th anniversary edition, 2018), 62.
31. David Hayward, "Christian Digital Soup Cartoon," NakedPastor.com, https://nakedpastor.com/products/christian-soup-digital-cartoon.
32. Becky Garrison, "Affirming Healthy Narcissism," *Spirituality & Health*, https://www.spiritualityhealth.com/affirming-healthy-narcissism.

7. Connecting in Community

1. Lauren Jackson, "People Want to Belong," "The Morning," *New York Times*, May 4, 2025, https://www.nytimes.com/2025/05/04/briefing/believing-faith-belonging.html.
2. For a spot-on analysis of this dynamic that looks to be signaling the death of writing on wine (and, I'd argue, beer, cider, and craft spirits, along with other verticals like wellness and spirituality), check out Carl Giavanti, "Turning the Tables on Becky Garrison," *Wine Industry Advisor*, March 24, 2025, https://wineindustryadvisor.com/2025/03/24/turning-the-tables-on-becky-garrison.
3. Ray Oldenburg, "Project for Public Spaces," December 31, 2008, https://www.pps.org/article/roldenburg.
4. Becky Garrison, "Free Spirited," *Edible Seattle*, https://www.edibleseattle.com/features/liquid-assets/free-spirited.
5. _____, "Kristof Farms: Creating Community with Cider and Wine," April 2, 2024, *Cidercraft Magazine*, https://cidercraftmag.com/kristof-farms-creating-community-with-cider-and-wine.
6. _____, "Connecting Persian Culture and Pinot Noir With the Momtazi Family," *SIP*, February 21, 2025, https://sipmagazine.com/connecting-persian-culture-and-pinot-noir-with-the-momtazi-family.
7. _____, "Raise a Glass to Immigrant Winemakers," *OnlySky*, July 25, 2025, https://onlys.ky/americas-immigrant-winemakers.
8. _____, "The Return of Community Ciders," *Beverage Master*, March 31, 2023, https://beverage-master.com/2023/05/the-return-of-community-ciders.
9. _____, "How to Turn a Wine Tasting into a Spiritual Experience," *Spirituality & Health*, https://www.spiritualityhealth.com/spiritual-wine-tasting-experience; "Creating Sustainable Communities with Craft Food," *PBSSoCal*, November 2, 2017, https://www.pbssocal.org/food-living/creating-sustainable-communities-with-craft-food; and "Tracing the Sacred Origins of Wine," Medium.com, August 31, 2022, https://medium.com/@becky_garrison/tracing-the-sacred-origins-of-wine-6c0f2791fd6f. These reflections are found at Becky Garrison, "Are Brewpubs and Tasting Rooms the Churches of the Future?" *OnlySky*, October 10, 2024, https://onlys.ky/brewpub-church-of-future.
10. Pickathon, https://pickathon.com.
11. Pink Martini Sing-Along, *The Square PDX*, July 24, 2021, https://www.thesquarepdx.org/event/pink-martini-concert-sing-along.
12. Becky Garrison, "The Power of Storytelling," Medium.com, December 17, 2022, https://medium.com/@becky_garrison/the-power-of-storytelling-e22c5e8c0131.
13. Kurt Neilson, email correspondence, April 1, 2025.
14. Emma Werner, "The 'Church' of CrossFit: PW Talks with Katie Rose Hejtmanek," *Publishers Weekly*, March 19, 2025, https://www.publishersweekly.com/pw/by-topic/industry-news/religion/article/97344-the-church-of-crossfit-pw-talks-with-katie-rose-hejtmanek.html.

15. Marc Maron, *Attempting Normal* (New York: Random House, 2014), Location 163, Kindle version.

16. Portions of this reflection were taken from Becky Garrison, "How to Find Healing by Connecting to Your Pre-Trauma Self," *Spirituality & Health*, https://www. spiritualityhealth.com/pre-trauma-self.

17. Thich Nhat Hanh, *How to Live When a Loved One Dies: Healing Meditations for Grief and Loss* (Berkeley, CA: Parallax Press, 2021), 54.

Appendix A: Spiritual Narcissism Case Study: Unpacking the History Behind Mars Hill Church's Missional Madness

1. The Mars Hill Church Saga was reposted to the *Gaslighting for God Substack* as a three-part series. See https://beckygarrison.substack.com/p/spiritual-narcissism-case-study-unpacking-731.

2. *The Door*, March/April 1992, Issue No. 122, graphic courtesy of wittenburgdoor.com.

3. See Jessica Johnson's research for an anthropological analysis of the Mars Hill Church saga, https://www.kuow.org/stories/the-rise-and-fall-of-a-seattle-megachurch-through-the-eyes-of-an-anthropologist.

4. Genevieve Carlton, "Legendary Pastors Who Fell From Grace," Ranker.com, January 25, 2025, https://www.ranker.com/list/pastors-that-fell-from-grace/genevieve-carlton.

5. Warren Throckmorton, "Nine Current Mars Hill Church Elders Take a Bold Stand," WThrockmorton.com, August 28, 2014, https://wthrockmorton.com/2014/08/28/nine-current-mars-hill-church-elders-take-a-bold-stand.

6. See Becky Garrison, "A 'Mixed Economy' of Church in a Post-Christian Marketplace," *Reflections*, Yale Divinity School (Fall 2009), https://reflections.yale.edu/article/how-firm-foundation-churches-face-future/mixed-economy-church-post-christian-marketplace.

7. See Brad Sargent, *Diagnosing Emergent*, https://diagnosingemergent.wordpress.com.

8. An earlier version of this experience is found at *Jesus Died for This?*, 185–189.

9. Warren Throckmorton, "Mark Driscoll," WThrockmorton.com, https://wthrockmorton.com/?s=Mark+Driscoll.

10. See Wenatchee the Hatchet, "A Page with an Index of Tagged Posts Discussing the History of the Former Mars Hill Church," https://wenatcheethehatchet.blogspot.com/p/a-page-with-index-of.html; and "Timeline," *Joyful Exiles*, https://joyfulexiles.com/timeline.

11. Sarah Eekhoff Zylstra, "How Acts 29 Survived—and Thrived—After the Collapse of Mars Hill," *The Gospel Coalition*, December 5, 2017, https://www.thegospelcoalition.org/article/how-acts-29-survived-and-thrived-after-the-collapse-of-mars-hill/?queryID=a55e4485f7b15ec75c140b5b98bd366d.

12. Acts 29, https://www.acts29.com.

13. See "Diagnosing the Emergent Movement, 04 Personal Issues Between Tony Jones and Julie MacMahon," *Diagnosing Emergent*, https://diagnosingemergent.wordpress.com/04-personal-issues-between-tony-jones-and-julie-mcmahon; and Libby Anne, "On Responding to Abuse Allegations," *Love, Joy, Feminism*, January 30, 2015, https://www.patheos.com/blogs/lovejoyfeminism/2015/01/on-responding-to-abuse-allegations.html.

14. Sian Ferguson, "What Ethical Non-Monogamy Is and Isn't," PsychCentral.com, July 28, 2021, https://psychcentral.com/health/ethical-non-monogamy-polyamory.

15. Brian McLaren, Tony Jones," https://brianmclaren.net/?s=Tony+Jones; and Tony Jones, "Recap of The Great Emergence National Event," Beliefnet.com, December 2008, https://www.beliefnet.com/columnists/tonyjones/2008/12/recap-of-the-great-emergence-n.html.

16. Becky Garrison, "Rise of the Party of Nones," *The Humanist*, May 26, 2019, https://thehumanist.com/commentary/rise-party-nones.

17. _____, "#Churchtoo," *The Baffler*, May 21, 2018, https://thebaffler.com/latest/churchtoo-garrison.

18. Brad Sargent, "Mars Hill Case Study: 02 Organizational System," *Futuristguy*, https://futuristguy.wordpress.com/mars-hill-case-study/02-organizational-system.

19. See "Full Comments on Tony Jones on Mark Driscoll—What Came First, the Thug or the Theology?" NakedPastor.com (archive copy) https://nakedpastor.com/blogs/news/tony-jones-on-mark-driscoll-what-came-first-the-thug-or-the-theology?srsltid=AfmBOoq8OGm07TPG4n8xOLnoUX2I1QwaXGN7YcSUjylX5pPASjW2CoL5.

20. "The Rise and Fall of Mars Hill Church," Episodes 1–19, *Christianity Today*, https://www.christianitytoday.com/podcasts/the-rise-and-fall-of-mars-hill.

21. "The Rise and Fall of Twin Hills," Parts 1–5, https://www.megathepodcast.com/p/rise-fall-of-twin-hills-mini-series.

22. See Daniel Silliman, "Sexual Harassment Went Unchecked at Christianity Today," *Christianity Today*, March 15, 2022, https://www.christianitytoday.com/2022/03/sexual-harassment-ct-guidepost-assessment-galli-olawoye.

23. Jaclyn Diaz, "The Scandal Roiling One of the Nation's Biggest Megachurches, Explained," *NPR*, June 27, 2024, https://www.npr.org/2024/06/24/nx-s1-5017881/robert-morris-gateway-church-sex-abuse-scandal-explained.

24. *The Door Magazine*, January/February 2002, Issue No. 179, graphic courtesy of wittenburgdoor.com.

25. Baptist Accountability, https://www.facebook.com/BaptistAccountability.

26. "EMERGED Podcast," *Homebrewed Christianity*, https://homebrewedchristianity.lpages.co/emerged-an-oral-history-of-the-emerging-church-movement.

27. Ryan Burge, "The Four Types of Nones," *Graphs About Religion*, https://www.graphsaboutreligion.com/p/the-four-types-of-nones.

28. The New Evangelicals, https://www.thenewevangelicals.com.

29. See Karl and Laura Forehand, "Special Edition—Spiritual Abuse—TNE, Tony Jones, and the Theo Bros," *The Desert Sanctuary*, August 24, 2023, https://thedesertsanctuary.org/2023/08/24/special-edition-spiritual-abuse-tne-tony-jones-and-the-theo-bros.

30. See Tony Jones, "Cancelled," *Tony's Field Notes*, February 6, 2025, https://substack.com/home/post/p-156010674; and Karl Forehand, "Organizations Come First—Tim Whitaker & The New Evangelicals," *Patheos*, March 20, 2025, https://www.patheos.com/blogs/thedesertsanctuary/2025/03/organizations-come-first-tim-whitaker-the-new-evangelicals.

31. Kimberly Winston, "Philosopher Says No to Major Science Forum Over Templeton Funding," *Religion News Service*, May 8, 2015, https://religionnews.com/2015/05/08/philosopher-says-no-major-science-forum-templeton-funding.

32. The New Evangelicals: GRACE Report, https://www.thenewevangelicals.com/grace-report.

33. William B. Eerdeman's Publishing Company, Marketing & Publicity Department, email correspondence, April 1, 2025.

34. See Karl Forehand, J. D. Forehand, Stuart Delony, with guest Megan Benninger, "Tim Whitaker & TNE—Not Getting It," Episode 21, *The Unlearning Curve Podcast*, https://open.spotify.com/episode/6SMfyTp9ZAygvO2c7qhv6j. Also, see Rick Pidcock, "That Time I Got an Angry Call from the Subject of an Article about Anger and Abuse," *Baptist News Global*, March 23, 2025, https://baptistnews.com/article/that-time-i-got-an-angry-call-from-the-subject-of-an-article-about-anger-and-abuse.

35. *Tim and April Show*, March 25, 2025, https://www.instagram.com/timandaprilshow/reel/DHo-rz-uK_f.

36. _____, April 11, 2025, https://www.instagram.com/timandaprilshow/p/DITxVpDumT.

37. Melissa Deckman, "The Real Religion Gen Z Story Is About Women," *Religion News Service*, March 7, 2025, https://religionnews.com/2025/03/07/the-real-gen-z-religion-story-is-about-women.

38. Rick Pidcock, "Allegations Against Tim Whitaker and The New Evangelicals Show How Hierarchy Transfers to Progressive Ministries," *Baptist News Global*, March 19, 2025, https://baptistnews.com/article/allegations-against-tim-whitaker-and-the-new-evangelicals-show-how-hierarchy-transfers-to-progressive-ministries.

39. Sargent, email correspondence.

40. Ibid.

41. Warren Throckmorton, Zoom interview, November 20, 2024.

42. See Wenatchee the Hatchet, "Nadia Bolz-Weber, Mark Driscoll 2.0 But for the Progressive Christian American," April 4, 2020, https://wenatcheethehatchet.blogspot.com/2020/04/nadia-bolz-weber-mark-driscoll-20-for.html.

Appendix B: Resources for Beginning the Healing Journey

1. Kathy Escobar, "A Thing (or 5) About Narcissism," KathyEscobar.com, November 17, 2021, https://kathyescobar.com/a-thing-or-5-about-narcissism.

Acknowledgments

1. Tia Leavings, *A Well Trained Wife: My Escape from Christian Patriarchy* (New York: St. Martin's Press), p 283.

2. See Becky Garrison, "Gary Austin: Making Surprising Sense," *Killing the Buddha*, November 13, 2013, https://killingthebuddha.com/ktblog/gary-austin-making-surprising-sense and Becky Garrison, "A Secular Grief Observed," *Killing the Buddha*, June 7, 2019, https://killingthebuddha.com/ktblog/a-secular-grief-observed.

About the Author

As a religious satirist, Becky Garrison served as senior contributing editor for *The Wittenburg Door* from 1994 to 2008, and has been on its board of directors since its relaunch in 2021. She's the author of nine books, including *Jesus Died for This? A Satirist's Search for the Risen Christ* and *Distilled in Washington: A History*. Also, she co-edited a book of love letters penned by partners of trans folks to their loved ones, as well as contributing chapters to about a dozen other books. She lives in the Pacific Northwest, where she covers the region's craft culture, including cider, beer, wine, spirits, cannabis/CBD, psychedelics, and the regional festival scene.

About Lake Drive Books

Lake Drive Books is an independent publishing company offering books that help you heal, grow, and discover. We champion books about values and strategies, not ideologies, and authors who are spiritually rich, contextually intelligent, and focused on human flourishing. We want to help readers feel seen.

If you like this or any of our other books at lakedrivebooks.com, we could use your help: please follow our authors on social media, subscribe to their newsletters, and tell others what you think of their remarkable books.